Video Data

INNOVATIVE TECHNOLOGY SERIES
INFORMATION SYSTEMS AND NETWORKS

Video Data

edited by
**Mohand-Saïd Hacid
& Salima Hassas**

HPS
HERMES PENTON SCIENCE

First published in 2000 by Hermes Science Publications, Paris
First published in 2002 by Hermes Penton Ltd
Derived from Networking and Information Systems Journal, *Video Data*, Vol. 3, no. 1.

Hermes Penton Science
120 Pentonville Road
London N1 9JN

British Library Cataloguing in Publication Data

A CIP record for this book is available from the British Library.

ISBN 1 9039 9622 8

Typeset by Saxon Graphics Ltd, Derby
Printed and bound in Great Britain by Biddles Ltd, Guildford and King's Lynn
www.biddles.co.uk

Contents

Foreword

With recent progress in computer technology and decreasing storage and processing costs, it is possible for computers to store huge amounts of video data. Whilst such media are widely used in today's communication (e.g., in the form of home movies, education and training, scholarly research), efficient storage, querying and navigation of video data are still lacking. Many databases need to be created to meet the increasing development of advanced applications such as video on demand, video/visual/multimedia databases, monitoring, virtual reality, Internet video, interactive TV, video conferencing, video e-mail, etc. These applications need new techniques and tools for managing video data. Video data management requires the contribution of many research disciplines and poses new research challenges to scientists and engineers. Image/video analysis and processing, pattern recognition and computer vision, multimedia data modelling, multidimensional indexing, man-machine interaction and data visualization, are only some of the more important research fields that contribute to this new area of research.

The following selected contributions cover some of the important issues in video management:

Augmented Transition Network as a Semantic Model for Video Data by Chen, Shyu and Kashyap addresses the issue of using an artificial intelligence technique, the ATN, to model in a single framework multimedia presentation, multimedia database searching, and browsing.

Spatio-temporal aspects are important in video databases. *Automatic Video Scene Segmentation Based on Spatial-Temporal Clues and Rhythm* by Mahdi, Ardebilian and Chen describes a new method for the capture of the semantic structure of video data by merging spatial, temporal and rhythm clues.

Database technology will play an important role in retrieving, integrating and correlating video data. *Dynamic Generation of Video Abstracts Using an Object-oriented Video DBMS* by Martin and Lozano is concerned with the use of a database approach to video retrieval and summarization.

Video segmentation is the topic of *Framework for Evaluation of Video-to-shots Segmentation Algorithms* by Ruiloba and Joly. This paper provides a framework in which temporal video segmentation algorithms can be analyzed and compared.

Synchronization is a problem notoriously hard to approach in multimedia applications. *Real-time Synchronization of Distributed Multimedia Applications* by Mouchawrab and Desbiens describes a new algorithm to ensure causal ordering of messages with real-time constraints in distributed multimedia applications.

Finally, *Active Bandwidth Sharing for Multi-layered Video in Multi-source Environments* by Achir, Dias de Amorim, Duarte and Pujolle deals with the issue of multi-source multicast distribution of multi-layered video.

Mohand-Saïd Hacid
Salima Hassas

Chapter 1

Augmented transition network as a semantic model for video data

Shu-Ching Chen
School of Computer Science, Florida International University, USA

Mei-Ling Shyu
Department of Electrical and Computer Engineering, University of Miami, USA

R.L. Kashyap
School of Electrical and Computer Engineering, Purdue University, USA

1. Introduction

Recently, multimedia database systems have emerged as a fruitful area for research due to recent progress in high-speed communication networks, large capacity storage devices, digitized media, and data compression technologies over the last few years. Multimedia information has been used in a variety of applications including manufacturing, education, medicine, entertainment, etc. Unlike the traditional database systems which have text or numerical data, a multimedia database or information system may contain different media such as text, image, audio, and video. The important characteristic of such a system is that all of the different media are brought together into one single unit, all controlled by a computer.

An increasing number of digital library systems allow users to access not only textual or pictorial documents, but also video data. Video is popular in many applications such as education and training, video conferencing, video on demand, news service, and so on. Digital library applications based on a huge amount of digital video data must be able to satisfy complex semantic information needs and require efficient browsing and searching mechanisms to extract relevant information [HOL 98]. Traditionally, when users want to search for certain content in videos, they need to fast forward or rewind to get a quick overview of interest on the video tape. This is a sequential process and users do not have a chance to choose or jump to a specific topic directly. In most cases, users have to browse through parts of the video collection to get the information they want, which address the contents and the meaning of the video documents. Also, users should have the opportunity to retrieve video materials by using database queries. Since video data contains rich semantic information, database queries should allow users to get high level content such as *scenes* or *shots* and low level content according to the temporal and spatial relations of semantic objects. A semantic object is an object appearing in a video frame, for example a "car". How to organize video data and provide the visual content in compact forms becomes important in multimedia applications [YEO 97]. Hence, a semantic model should have the ability to model visual contents at different granularities so that users can quickly browse large video collections.

With the emerging demand for content-based video processing approaches, more and more attention is devoted to segmenting video frames into regions such that each region, or a group of regions, corresponds to an object that is meaningful to human viewers [FER 97, COU 97]. This kind of object-based representation of the video data is being incorporated into standards like MPEG4 and MPEG7 [FER 97]. A video clip is a temporal sequence of two-dimensional samples of the visual field. Each sample is an image which is referred to as a *frame* of the video. Segmentation of an image, in its most general sense, is to divide it into smaller parts. In image segmentation, the input image is partitioned into regions such that each region satisfies some homogeneity criterion. The regions, which are usually characterized by homogeneity criteria like intensity values, texture, etc., are also referred to as *classes*. Video segmentation is a very important step in processing video clips. One of the emerging applications in video processing is its storage and retrieval from multimedia databases and content-based indexing. Video data can be temporally segmented into smaller groups depending on the scene activity where each group contains several frames. Clips are divided into *scenes* and scenes into *shots*. A shot is considered the smallest group of frames that represent a semantically consistent unit.

Videos include verbal and visual information that is spatially, graphically, and temporally spread out. This makes indexing video data more complex than textual data. Typically, indexing covers only the topical or content-dependent characteristics. The extra-topical or content-independent characteristics of visual information are not indexed. These characteristics include color, texture, or objects represented in a picture that topical indexing would not include, but which users may rely on when making relevance judgments [KOM 98]. Hence, it is very important to provide the users with such visual cues in browsing. For this purpose, *key frames* extracted from the videos are one of the means of providing visual surrogates of video data.

Many video browsing models propose to provide the facility for users to visualize video content based on user interactions [ARM 94, DAY 95, FLI 95, MIL 92, OOM 93, SMO 94, YEO 97]. These models choose representative images using regular time intervals, one image in each shot, all frames with a focus key frame at a specific place, and so on. Choosing key frames based on regular time intervals may miss some important segments and segments may have multiple key frames with similar contents. One image in each shot also may not capture the temporal and spatial relations of semantic objects. Showing all key frames may confuse users when too many key frames are displayed at the same time. To achieve a balance, we propose a key frame selection mechanism based on the number, temporal, and spatial changes of the semantic objects in the video frames.

The *augmented transition network (ATN)*, developed by Woods [WOO 70], has been used in natural language understanding systems and question answering systems for both text and speech. We use the ATN as semantic model-to-model multimedia presentations [CHE 97a], multimedia database searching, the temporal, spatial, or spatio-temporal relations of various media streams and semantic objects [CHE 97b, SHY 98]. As shown in [CHE 97c], ATNs need fewer nodes and arcs to represent a multimedia presentation compared with Petri-net models such as OCPN [LIT 90]. Multimedia input strings adopt the notations from regular expressions [KLE 56] and are used to represent the presentation sequences of temporal media streams, spatio-temporal relations of semantic objects, and keyword compositions. In addition to using ATNs to model multimedia presentations and multimedia database searching, how to use ATNs and multimedia input strings as video browsing models is discussed in this paper. Moreover, key frame selection based on the temporal and spatial relations of semantic objects in each shot will be discussed. In previous studies, formulations and algorithms for multiscale image segmentation and unsupervised video segmentation and object tracking were introduced [KAS 98, SIS 99a, SIS 99b]. Our video segmentation method focuses on obtaining object level segmentation, i.e., obtaining objects in each frame and their traces across the frames. Hence, the temporal and spatial relations of semantic objects required in the proposed key frame selection mechanism can be captured. We apply our video segmentation method on a small portion of a soccer game video and use the temporal and spatial relations of semantic objects to illustrate how the key frame selection mechanism works.

The organization of this paper is as follows. Section 2 discusses the use of ATNs and multimedia input strings to model video browsing. The key frame selection algorithm is introduced in Section 3. Section 3 also gives an example of a soccer game video. Conclusions are presented in Section 4.

2. Video browsing using ATNs

In an interactive multimedia information system, users should have the flexibility to browse and decide on various scenarios they want to see. This means that two-way communications should be captured by the conceptual model. Digital video has gained increasing popularity in many multimedia applications. Instead of sequential access to the video content, structuring and modeling video data so that users can quickly and easily browse and retrieve interesting materials becomes an important issue in designing multimedia information systems.

Browsing provides users with the opportunity to view information rapidly since they can choose the content relevant to their needs. It is similar to the table of contents and the index of a book. The advantage is that users can quickly locate the interesting topic and avoid the sequential and time-consuming process. In a digital video library, in order to provide this capability, a semantic model should allow users to navigate a video stream based on shots, scenes, or clips. The ATN can be used to model the spatio-temporal relations of multimedia presentations and multimedia database systems. It allows users to view part of a presentation by issuing database queries. In this paper, we further design a mechanism by using the ATN to model video browsing so that users can navigate the video contents. In this manner, querying and browsing capabilities can be provided by using ATNs.

2.1. Hierarchy for a video clip

As mentioned in [YEO 97], a video clip can be divided into *scenes*. A *scene* is a common event or locale which contains a sequential collection of *shots*. A *shot* is a basic unit of video production which captures between a record and a stop camera operation. Figure 1 shows a hierarchy for a video clip. At the topmost level is the video clip. A clip contains several *scenes* at the second level and each *scene* contains several *shots*. Each *shot* contains some contiguous *frames* which are at the lowest level in the video hierarchy. Since a video clip may contain many video frames, it is not good for database retrieving and browsing. How to model a video clip, based on different granularities, to accommodate browsing, searching and retrieval at different levels is an important issue in multimedia database and information systems. A video hierarchy can be defined by the following three properties:

1. $V = \{S_1, S_2, ..., S_N\}$, S_i denotes the ith scene and N is the number of scenes in this video clip. Let $B(S_1)$ and $E(S_1)$ be the starting and ending times of scene

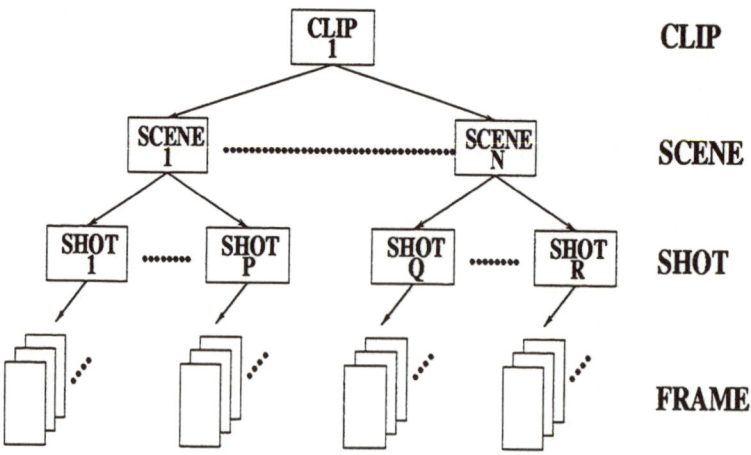

Figure 1. A hierarchy of video media stream

S_1, respectively. The temporal relation $B(S_1) < E(S_1) < B(S_2) < E(S_2)B < ...$ is preserved.

2. $S_i = \{T_1^i, ..., T_{ni}^i\}$, T_j^i is the jth shot in scene S_i and n_i is the number of shots in S_i. Let $B(T_1^i)$ and $E(T_1^i)$ be the starting and ending times of shot T_1^i where $B(T_1^i) < E(T_1^i) < ... < B(T_{ni}^i) < E(T_{ni}^i)$.

3. $T_j^i = \{R_1^{i,j}, ..., R_{lj}^{i,j}\}$, $R_1^{i,j}$ and $R_{lj}^{i,j}$ are the starting and ending frames in shot T_j^i and lj is the number of frames for shot T_j^i.

In property 1, V represents a video clip and contains one or more *scene* denoted by S_1, S_2, and so on. *Scenes* follow a temporal order. For example, the ending time of S_1 is earlier than the starting time of S_2. As shown in property 2, each *scene* contains some *shots* such as T_1^i to T_{ni}^i. *Shots* also follow a temporal order and there is no time overlap among shots so $B(T_1^i) < E(T_1^i) < ... < B(T_{ni}^i) < E(T_{ni}^i)$. A *shot* contains some key frames to represent the visual contents and changes in each shot. In property 3, $R_k^{i,j}$ represents key frame k for shot T_j^i. The details of how to choose key frames based on temporal and spatial relations of semantic objects in each shot will be discussed in Section 3.

2.2. Using ATNs to model video browsing

An ATN can build up the hierarchy property by using its subnetworks. Figure 2 is an example of how to use an ATN and its subnetworks to represent a video hierarchy. An ATN and its subnetwork are capable of segmenting a video clip into different granularities and still preserve the temporal relations of different units.

Table 1 shows the traces of ATN for presentation V in Figure 2. This table is used to explain how ATN works for video browsing. The part of the steps are shown as follows:

Step 1: The current state is V and the arc to be followed is arc number 1 with arc label V_1. The input symbol V_1 is a subnetwork name (as shown in Figure 2(b)). Since input symbol V_1 (video clip) is a subnetwork name, the state name (V/V_1) at the head of arc 1 is put into a stack which is shown at backup states in Table 1. The control passes to the subnetwork V_1 (Figure 2(b)) after the state name is put into the stack.

Step 2: The current state is $V_1/$ which is the starting state of a subnetwork as shown in Figure 2(b). Arc number 2 is followed and the arc label is $S_1\&S_2$. Arc label $S_1\&S_2$ means a video clip V_1 consists of two scenes to let users choose and they are S_1 and S_2. Assuming the user chooses S_1, arc number 4 is followed and the arc label (input symbol) is S_1. Since S_1 is also a subnetwork name, the state name V_1/S_1 at the head of this arc is pushed into the stack so that this state name is on top of the state name V/V_1. Therefore, there are two state names in the stack at this stage. The control passes to the subnetwork in Figure 2(c).

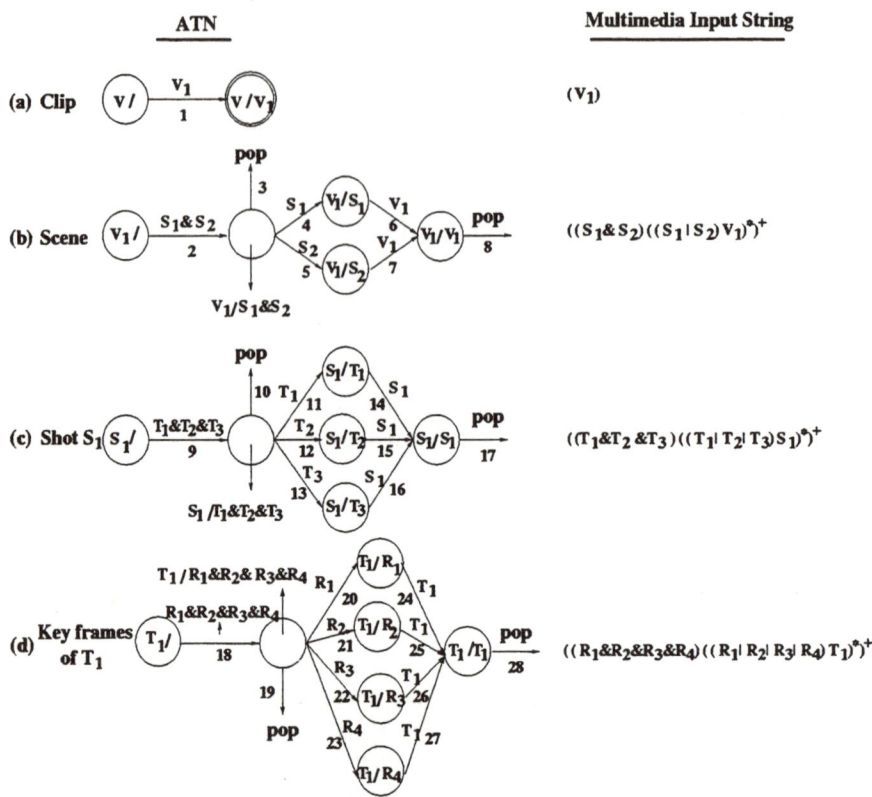

Figure 2. *Augmented Transition Network for video browsing: (a) is the ATN network for a video clip which starts at the state V/. (b)–(d) are part of the subnetworks of (a). (b) is to model scenes in video clip V1. (c) is to model shots in scene S_1. Key frames for shot T_1 is in (d).*

Step 3: The current state is $S_1/$. Arc number 9 with arc label $T_1\&T_2\&T_3$ is followed. This arc label indicates that scene S_1 consists of three shots: T_1, T_2, and T_3.

In Figure 2(a), the arc label V_1 is the starting state name of its subnetwork in Figure 2(b). When the input symbol V_1 is read, the name of the state at the head of the arc (V/V_1) is pushed into the top of a push-down store. The control is then passed to the state named on the arc which is the subnetwork in Figure 2(b).

In Figure 2(b), when the input symbol X_1 $(S_1\&S_2)$ is read, two frames which represent two video scenes S_1 and S_2 are both displayed for the selections. In the original video sequence, S_1 appears earlier than S_2 since it has a smaller number. The "&" symbol in multimedia input strings is used to denote the concurrent display of S_1 and S_2. ATNs are capable of modeling user interactions where

Table 1. *The trace of ATN for the browsing sequence in Figure 2*

Step	Current State	Input Symbol	Arc Followed	Backup States
1	$V/$	V_1	1	V/V_1
2	$V_1/$	$S_1\&S_2$	2	V/V_1
3	$V_1/S_1\&S_2$	S_1	4	V_1/S_1 V/V_1
4	$S_1/$	$T_1\&T_2\&T3$	9	V_1/S_1 V/V_1
5	$S_1/T_1\&T_2\&T3$	T_1	12	S_1/T_1 V_1/S_1 V/V_1
6	$T_1/$	$R_1\&R_2\&R3\&R_4$	18	S_1/T_1 V_1/S_1 V/V_1
7	$T_1/R_1\&R_2\&R3\&R_4$	R_1	20	S_1/T_1 V_1/S_1 V/V_1
8	T_1/R_1	T_1	24	T_1/T_1 S_1/T_1 V_1/S_1 V/V_1
9	$T_1/$	$R_1\&R_2\&R_3\&R_4$	18	S_1/T_2 V_1/S_1 V/V_1
10	$T_1/R_1\&R_2\&R_3\&R_4$	None	19	V_1/S_1 V/V_1
11	S_1/T_2	S_1	15	S_1/S_1 V_1/S_1 V/V_1
12	$S_1/$	$T_1\&T_2\&T_3$	9	S_1/S_1 V_1/S_1 V/V_1
13	$S_1/T_1\&T_2\&T_3$	None	10	V_1/S_1 V/V_1
14	S_1/S_1	None	17	V/V_1
15	V_1/S_1	V_1	6	V_1/V_1 V/V_1
16	$V_1/$	$S_1\&S_2$	2	V_1/V_1 V/V_1
17	$V_1/S_1\&S_2$	None	3	V/V_1
18	V_1/V_1	None	8	NIL
19	Finish			

different selections will go to different states so that users have the opportunity to directly jump to the specific video unit that they want to see. In our design, vertical bars " | " in multimedia input strings and more than one outgoing arc in each state at ATNs are used to model the "or" condition so that user interactions are allowed. Assume S_1 is selected, the input symbol S_1 is read. Control is passed to the subnetwork in Figure 2(c) with starting state name $S_1/$. The "*" symbol indicates that the selection is optional for the users since it may not be activated if users want to stop browsing. The subnetwork for S_2 is omitted for the simplicity.

In Figure 2(c), when the input symbol $T_1\&T_2\&T_3$ is read, three frames T_1, T_2, and T_3. which represent three shots of scene S_1 are displayed for the selection. If the shot T_1 is selected, the control will be passed to the subnetwork in Figure 2(d) based on the arc symbol $T_1/$. As in Figure 2(b), temporal flow is maintained.

3. The proposed key frame selection approach

The next level under *shots* are key frames. Key frame selections play an important role to let users examine the key changes in each video shot. Since each shot may still have too many video frames, it is reasonable to use key frames to represent the *shots*. The easiest way of key frame selection is to choose the first frame of the shot. However, this method may miss some important temporal and spatial changes in each shot. The second way is to include all video frames as key frames and this may have computational and storage problems, and may increase users' perception burdens. The third way is to choose key frames based on fixed durations. This method is still not a good mechanism since it may give us many key frames with similar contents. Therefore, how to select key frames to represent a video *shot* is an important issue for digital library browsing, searching, and retrieval [YEU 95]. To achieve a balance, we propose a key frame selection mechanism based on the number, temporal, and spatial changes of the semantic objects in the video frames. Other features may also be possible for the key frame selections, but we focus on the number, temporal, and spatial relations of semantic objects in this study. Therefore, spatio-temporal changes in each shot can be represented by these key frames. For example, in each shot of a soccer game, players may change positions in subsequent frames and the number of players appearing may change at the time duration of the shot.

3.1. Simultaneous partition and class parameter estimation (SPCPE) algorithm

Let the set of semantic objects in the kth frame ($R_k^{i,j}$) of the jth shot T_j^i in the ith scene S_i be denoted by $O_k^{i,j}$ We define the key frame selections as follows:

Definition 1: Given two contiguous video frames $R_a^{i,j}$ and $R_b^{i,j}$ in T_j^i, let the sets of the semantic objects in these two video frames be $O_a^{i,j}$ and $O_b^{i,j}$. $R_b^{i,j}$ is a key frame if and only if any of following two conditions is satisfied:

(1) $O_a^{i,j} \cap O_b^{i,j} \neq O_a^{i,j} \cup O_b^{i,j}$;

(2) Any semantic object spatial location changes between $O_a^{i,j}$ and $O_b^{i,j}$.

As mentioned previously, the video segmentation method can provide the information required for the key frame selection mechanism. Therefore, the video segmentation method is applied to each frame before the above two conditions are checked. The method of partitioning a video frame starts with an arbitrary partition and employs an iterative algorithm to estimate the partition and the class description parameters jointly. So the minimum we obtain through our descent method depends strongly on the starting point or the initial partition. In a video, the successive frames do not differ much due to the high temporal sampling rate. Hence the partitions of adjacent frames do not differ significantly. Starting with the estimated partition of the previous frame, if we apply our descent algorithm on the current frame we may obtain a new partition that is not significantly different from the partition of the previous frame. For the first frame, since there is no previous frame, we use a randomly generated initial partition.

We treat the partition as well as the class parameters as random variables and pose the problem as one in joint estimation [KAS 98, SIS 99a]. Suppose there are two classes. Let the two classes be described by the probability densities denoted by $p_1(y_{ij})$ and $p_2(y_{ij})$. Also, let the partition variable be $c = \{c_1, c_2\}$ and the classes be parameterized by $\theta = \{\theta_1, \theta_2\}$. Consider an image of N_r rows and N_c columns (i.e., image of size $N_r \times N_c$) with intensities given by $Y = \{y_{ij} : 1 \le i \le N_r, 1 \le j \le N_c\}$. We estimate the best partition as that which maximizes the a posteriori probability (MAP) of the partition variable given the image data Y. Now, the MAP estimates of $c = \{c_1, c_2\}$ and $\theta = \{\theta_1, \theta_2\}$ are given by:

$$(\hat{c}, \hat{\theta}) = \underset{(c,\theta)}{\text{Arg max}}\ P(c, \theta \mid Y) = \underset{(c,\theta)}{\text{Arg max}}\ P(Y \mid c, \theta) P(c, \theta). \qquad [1]$$

Let $J(c, \theta)$ denote the function that needs to be minimized, i.e., the sum of terms. With appropriate assumptions, this joint estimation can be simplified to the following form:

$$(\hat{c}, \hat{\theta}) = \underset{(c,\theta)}{\text{Arg min}}\ J(c_1, c_2, \theta_1, \theta_2)$$

$$J(c_1, c_2, \theta_1, \theta_2) = \sum_{y_{ij} \in c_1} -\ln p_1(y_{ij}; \theta_1) + \sum_{y_{ij} \in c_2} -\ln p_2(y_{ij}; \theta_2). \qquad [2]$$

The joint estimation method is called the *simultaneous partition and class parameter estimation (SPCPE)* algorithm. The algorithm starts with an arbitrary partition of the data and computes the corresponding class parameters. Using these class parameters and the data a new partition is estimated. Both the partition and the class parameters are iteratively refined until there is no further change in them. The details of the video segmentation method are shown in [SIS 99b].

Given a video shot T_j^i, let K_j^i be the set of key frames selected for T_j^i and m a frame index. Initially the first frame is always selected so $K_j^i = \{R_1^{i,j}\}$.

1. Initialization:

- $K_j^i = \{R_1^{i,j}\}$;
- Execute SPCPE algorithm for the first frame;

2. for $m = 2$ to l_j

- Execute SPCPE algorithm to get the temporal and spatial relations of the semantic objects;
- if ($(O_m^{i,j} \cap O_{m-1}^{i,j} \neq O_m^{i,j} \cup O_{m-1}^{i,j})$ OR

  Spatial_location_change$(O_m^{i,j}, O_{m-1}^{i,j})$) then

  $K_j^i = K_j^i \cup R_m^{i,j}$;

  endfor;

The first condition of definition 1 models the number of semantic object changes in two contiguous video frames with the same shot. The first part of the if-statement in the above solution algorithm is used to check this situation. The latter part of the if-statement checks the second condition of definition 1, which is to model the temporal and spatial changes of semantic objects in two contiguous video frames of the shot. Using the same definition of three-dimensional relative positions for semantic objects as shown in [CHE 97b], we choose one semantic object to be the target semantic object in each video frame. We adopt the minimal bounding rectangle (MBR) concept in R-tree [GUT 84] so that each semantic object is covered by a rectangle. In order to distinguish the relative positions, twenty-seven numbers are used to distinguish the relative positions of each semantic object relative to the target semantic object and are represented by subscripted numbers. The centroid point of each semantic object is used for space reasoning so that any semantic object is mapped to a point object. Therefore, the relative position between the target semantic object and a semantic object can be derived from these centroid points.

3.2. Implementation and results

The example soccer video consists of 60 frames. It is a gray scale video that shows the part of the game where a goal is scored. Each frame is of size 180 rows and 240 columns. A small portion of the soccer video game is used to illustrate the way the proposed key frame selection mechanism works. Although we have several distinct regions in each frame of the video, only two of them are important from the content-based retrieval perspective, namely the ball and the players.

There are some important aspects in this video that make automatic object tracking difficult. They are as follows:

– The soccer ball vanishes between players for a few frames and reappears later.

– The regions corresponding to the players merge together and separate out after a few frames.

– Some spurious patches, typically on the ground, suddenly appear as blobs and disappear giving the impression of an object.

We will apply our video segmentation method to this data, assuming that there are two classes. The first frame is partitioned using the multiscale frame segmentation with two classes. The algorithm is initialized with a random starting partition. After obtaining the partition of the first frame, we compute the partitions of the subsequent frames. From the results on frames 1 through 60, a few frames – 1, 5, 8 and 13 – are shown in Figure 3 along with the original frames adjacent to them. As can be seen from Figure 3, the players, the soccer ball and the sign boards in the background (JVC, Canon, etc.) are all captured by a single class. The ground in the soccer field is captured by another class. Some of the players who are close together have been combined into a single segment. Similarly, the ball is merged into a single segment with two other players. For example, in frame 1, the ball and two players are part of one segment; whereas by the fifth frame, the soccer ball is far away so that it becomes a segment in itself. This continues until it goes in between two other players. Notice the patch on the ground which was near the right most player in the first frame that moves to the left uniformly owing to the camera panning to the right. In frame 5 we can see a spurious patch appearing out of nowhere. On the whole, the initial conditions from the previous frames seem to be guiding the segmentation of the current frame in an effective manner. There are some artifacts on the ground, specifically the one closest to the rightmost player, which show up as patches in the final partition. Inspection of the other frames shows that it is also present in them and not something spurious.

The segments of frame 1, extracted by applying the seeding and region growing method are shown in Figure 3(b). There are 15 segments in this frame out of which only 5 correspond to the players and the ball. The ball and 2 players are merged into one segment, and there are 2 other segments where two players are put into a single segment. The rest of the two segments consists of one player in each segment. We have implemented the programs to find the bounding boxes and the centroids for the segments. Therefore, the segments are displayed with the bounding boxes around them and the centroids are marked with an 'x' in Figure 3(b). The small segments with only a centroid and without any apparent bounding box are the ones with very few pixels. Most of them are on the top of the frame and at the bottom of the sign boards. They arise out of smoothing the broken soccer boundary line.

Since only the ball and the players are important from the content-based retrieval perspective, we use Figure 4 to simplify the segments for each frame. As

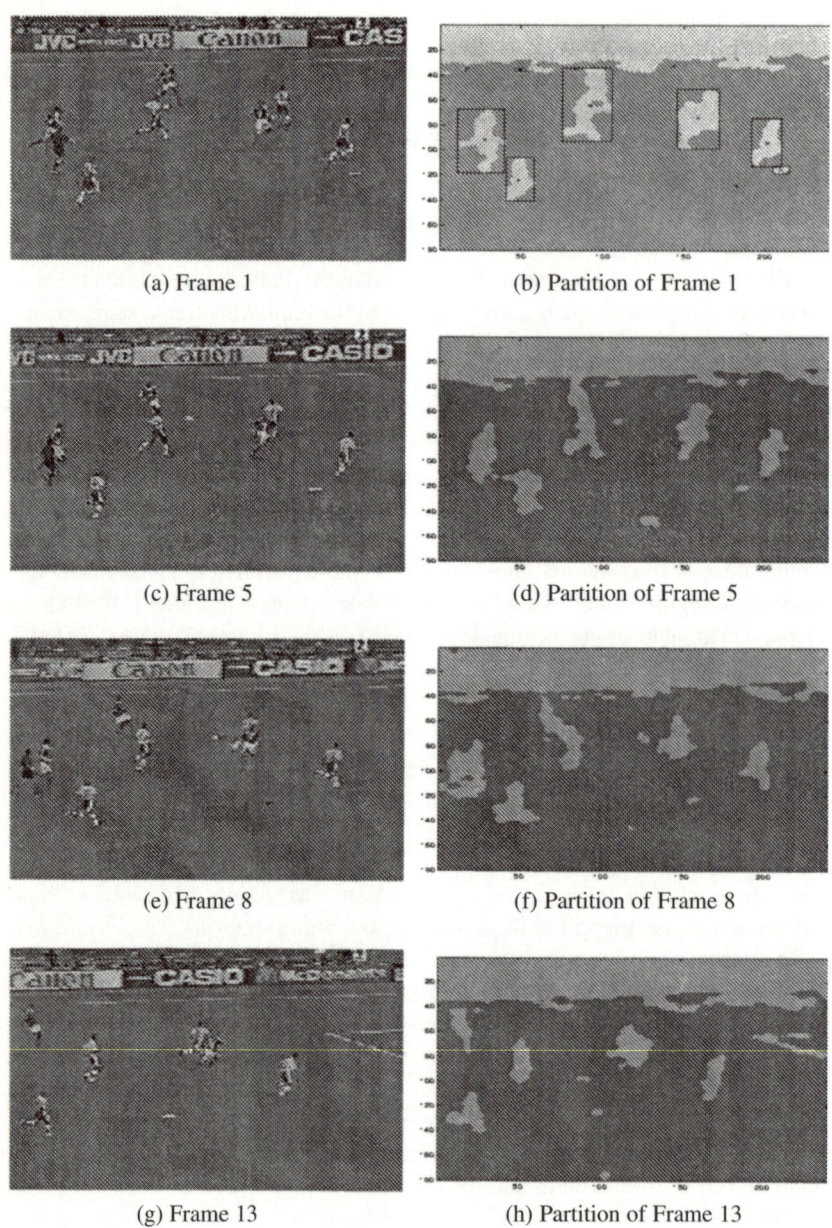

(a) Frame 1

(b) Partition of Frame 1

(c) Frame 5

(d) Partition of Frame 5

(e) Frame 8

(f) Partition of Frame 8

(g) Frame 13

(h) Partition of Frame 13

Figure 3. *Figures (a), (c), (e), (g) are the original Frames 1, 5, 8 13 (on the left) and (b), (d), (f), (h) show their corresponding partitions (on the right). (b) shows the segments extracted from the first frame of the soccer video. The centroid of each segment is marked with an 'x' and the segment is shown with a bounding box around it. The segments corresponding to the moving players and the ball are captured in every frame automatically.*

shown in Figure 4, the ground (**G**) is selected as the target semantic object and the segments are denoted by **P** for the players or **B** for the soccer ball. As mentioned earlier, if two semantic objects are too close to each other, they are merged into a single segment. Hence, the soccer ball is put into a single segment only when it is far away from the players (in frames 5 and 8) and each segment **P** may consist of multiple players and/or the soccer ball. In this example, each frame is divided into nine subregions. More or fewer subregions in a video frame may be used to allow more fuzzy or more precise queries as necessary. The corresponding multimedia input strings are on the right of Figure 4. In our design, each key frame is represented by an input symbol in a multimedia input string and the "&" symbol between two semantic objects is used to denote that the semantic objects appear in the same frame. The subscripted numbers are used to distinguish the relative positions of the semantic objects relative to the target semantic object "ground". Table 2 shows part of the three-dimensional spatial relations introduced in [CHE 97b]. (X_t, Y_t, Z_t) and (X_s, Y_s, Z_s) represent the X-, Y-, and Z-coordinates of the target and any semantic object, respectively. The "$\approx$" symbol means the difference between two coordinates is within a threshold value. Since two dimensions are considered in this example, $Z_s \approx Z_t$. The multimedia input strings can be used for multimedia database searching via substring matching. The details of multimedia database searching are shown in [CHE 97b].

Assume that Figures 4(a), (b), (c), and (d) are four key frames for shot T_1. The multimedia inpur string to represent these four key frames is as follows:

Multimedia input string:

$$\underbrace{(G_1 \& P_{10} \& P_{13} \& P_1 \& P_1 \& P_{19})}_{M_1} \underbrace{(G_1 \& P_{10} \& P_{13} \& P_1 \& B_1 \& P_1 \& P_{19})}_{M_2}$$
$$\underbrace{(G_1 \& P_{10} \& P_{13} \& P_{10} \& B_1 \& P_1 \& P_{19})}_{M_3} \underbrace{(G_1 \& P_{16} \& P_{13} \& P_{10} \& P_1 \& P_{19})}_{M_4}$$

As shown in the above multimedia input string, there are four input symbols which are M_1, M_2, M_3 and M_4. The appearance sequence of the semantic objects in an input symbol is based on the spatial locations of the semantic objects in the video frame from left to right and top to bottom. For example, Figure 4(a) is represented by input symbol M_1. G_1 indicates that **G** is the target semantic object, P_{10} means the first **P** is on the left of **G**, P_1 means the second **P** is below and to the left of **G**, P_1 means the third **P** and the fourth **P** are at the same subregion as **G**, and P_{19} means the fifth **P** is on the right of **G**. Figure 4(b) is modeled by input symbol M_2 in which the soccer ball **B** appears at the same subregion as **G** and the rest of the semantic objects remain at the same locations. In this case, the number of semantic objects is increased from six to seven. This is an example to show how to use a multimedia input string to represent a number of semantic object changes. Figure 4(c) is represented by input symbol M_3. The third **P** moves from

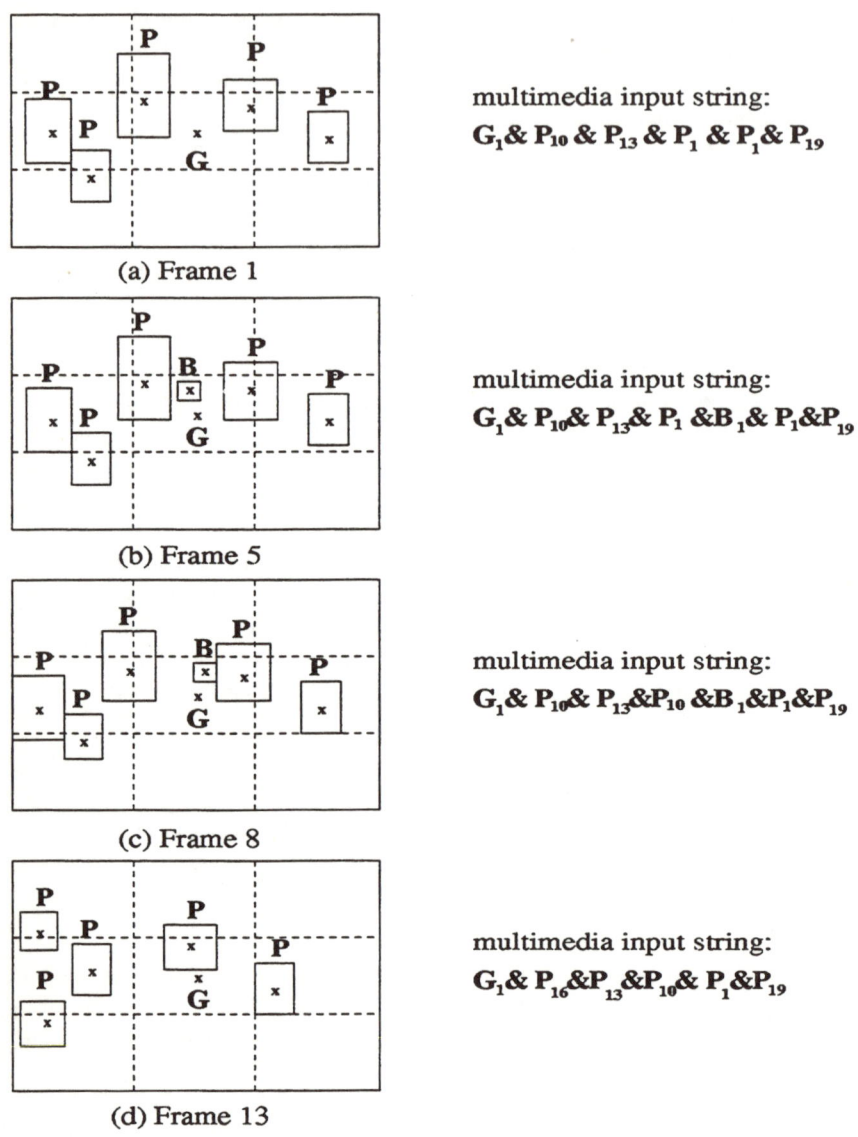

multimedia input string:
G_1 & P_{10} & P_{13} & P_1 & P_1 & P_{19}

(a) Frame 1

multimedia input string:
G_1 & P_{10} & P_{13} & P_1 & B_1 & P_1 & P_{19}

(b) Frame 5

multimedia input string:
G_1 & P_{10} & P_{13} & P_{10} & B_1 & P_1 & P_{19}

(c) Frame 8

multimedia input string:
G_1 & P_{16} & P_{13} & P_{10} & P_1 & P_{19}

(d) Frame 13

Figure 4. *Segments with bounding boxes and centroids for Frames 1, 5, 8, 13 in Figure 3 on the left and their corresponding multimedia input strings on the right. Each segment is displayed with the bounding box around it and the centroid is marked with an 'x'. Here, **G, P**, and **B** represent "ground", "players", and "soccer ball", respectively. The "ground" (**G**) is selected as the target semantic object and the subscripted numbers in a multimedia input string are used to distinguish the relative positions of the semantic objects relative to **G**. Each frame is divided into nine subregions and the centroid of each segment is used as a reference point for spatial reasoning.*

Table 2. *Part of the three-dimensional relative positions for semantic objects: The first and the third columns indicate the relative position numbers while the second and the fourth columns are the relative coordinates. (x_t, y_t, z_t) and (x_s, y_s, z_s) represent the X-, Y-, and Z-coordinates of the target and any semantic object, respectively. The "$\approx$" symbol means the difference between two coordinates is within a threshold value.*

Number	Relative Coordinates
1	$x_s \approx x_t, y_s \approx y_t, z_s \approx z_t$
10	$x_s < x_t, y_s \approx y_t, z_s \approx z_t$
13	$x_s < x_t, y_s < y_t, z_s \approx z_t$
16	$x_s < x_t, y_s > y_t, z_s \approx z_t$
19	$x_s > x_t, y_s \approx y_t, z_s \approx z_t$

the same subregion of **G** to above and left of **G** so the associated number changes from 1 to 10 from which the relative spatial relations can also be modeled by the multimedia input string. Input symbol M_4 models Figure 4(d). In this situation, **B** disappears and the first **P** changes its spatial location from the left to above and left of **G** in Figure 4(c). So, the number associated with the first **P** changes from 10 to 16 and **B** does not exist in M_4. The order of these four key frames is modeled by four input symbols concatenated together to indicate that M_1 appears earlier than M_2 and so on.

4. Conclusions

Video data are widely used in today's multimedia applications such as education, video on demand, video conferencing and so on. Managing video data so that users can quickly browse video data is an important issue for multimedia applications using video data. A good semantic model is needed if we want to meet the needs. In this paper, ATNs are used to model video hierarchy for browsing. Based on this design, users can view information quickly to decide whether the content is what they want to see. Key frames selection based on temporal and spatial relations of semantic objects is used in our design. The temporal and spatial relations of semantic objects are captured by the proposed unsupervised video segmentation method. From the soccer game video example, we can see that the players and the soccer ball are captured well. Since the first frame uses a random initialization and the subsequent frames use the results of the previous frames, the method is completely unsupervised. In addition, by incorporating the partition information of the previous frame into the segmentation process of the current frame, the temporal information is implicitly used. Under this design, these key frames preserve many of the visual contents and minimize the data size to mitigate the computation and storage problems in multimedia browsing environments. Moreover, based on the results of the segmentation, multimedia input strings are constructed. The multimedia input strings can be used for multimedia database searching via substring matching. Unlike the existing semantic models which only model presentation, query, or browsing, our ATN model provides these three capabilities in one framework.

Acknowledgements

This work has been partially supported by National Science Foundation under contract IRI 9619812.

REFERENCES

[ARM 94] ARMAN F., DEPOMMER R., HSU A., CHIU M.Y., "Content-based Browsing of Video Sequences", *ACM Multimedia 94*, p. 97–103, August 1994.

[CHE 97a] CHEN S.-C., KASHYAP R.L., "Temporal and Spatial Semantic Models for Multimedia Presentations", in *1997 International Symposium on Multimedia Information Processing*, p. 441–446, December 11–13, 1997.

[CHE 97b] CHEN S.-C., KASHYAP R.L., "A Spatio-Temporal Semantic Model for Multimedia Presentations and Multimedia Database Systems", accepted for publication *IEEE Transactions on Knowledge and Data Engineering*, 2000.

[CHE 97c] CHEN S.-C., KASHYAP R.L., "Empirical Studies of Multimedia Semantic Models for Multimedia Presentations", in *13th International Conference on Computers and Their Applications*, p. 226–229, March 25–27, 1998.

[COU 97] COURTNEY J.D., "Automatic Video Indexing via Object Motion Analysis", *Pattern Recognition*, vol. 30, no. 4, p. 607–625, 1997.

[DAY 95] DAY Y.F., DAGTAS S., IINO M., KHOKHAR A., GHAFOOR A., "Object-Oriented Concept Modeling of Video Data", *IEEE Int'l Conference on Data Engineering*, p. 401–408, March 1995.

[FER 97] FERMAN A.M., GUNSEL B., TEKALP A.M., "Object Based Indexing of MPEG-4 Compressed Video", in *Proc. SPIE: VCIP*, p. 953–963, vol. 3024, San Jose, USA, February 1997.

[FLI 95] FLICKNER M., SAWHNEY H., NIBLACK W., ASHLEY J., HUANG Q., DOM B., GORKANI M., HAFNER J., LEE D., PETKOVIC D., STEELE D., YANKER P., "Query by Image and Video Content: The QBIC System", *IEEE Computer*, vol. 28, no. 9, p. 23–31, September 1995.

[GUT 84] GUTTMAN A., "R-tree: A Dynamic Index Structure for Spatial Search", in *Proc. ACM SIGMOD*, p. 47–57, June 1984.

[HOL 98] HOLLFELDER S., EVERTS A., THIEL U., "Concept-Based Browsing in Video Libraries", *Proceedings of the IEEE Forum on Research and Technology Advances in Digital Libraries*, 1998.

[KAS 98] KASHYAP R.L. and SISTA S., "Unsupervised Classification and Choice of Classes: Bayesian Approach", Technical Report TR-ECE 98–12, School of Electrical and

Computer Engineering, Purdue University, July 1998.

[KLE 56] KLEENE S.C., "Representation of Events in Nerve Nets and Finite Automata, Automata Studies", *Princeton University Press*, Princeton, NJ., p. 3–41, 1956.

[KOM 98] KOMLODI A. and SLAUGHTER L., "Visual Video Browsing Interfaces Using Key Frames", *Proceedings of the CHI 98 Summary Conference on CHI 98 Summary: Human Factors in Computing Systems*, p. 337–338, 1998.

[LIT 90] LITTLE T.D.C., GHAFOOR A., "Synchronization and Storage Models for Multimedia Objects", *IEEE J. Selected Areas in Commun.*, vol. 9, p. 413–427, April 1990.

[MIL 92] MILLS M., COHEN J., WONG Y.Y., "A Magnifier Tool for Video Data", in *Proc. ACM Computer Human Interface (CHI)*, May 1992, p. 93–98.

[OOM 93] OOMOTO E., TANAKA K., "OVID: Design and Implementation of a Video Object Database System", *IEEE Trans. on Knowledge and Data Engineering*, vol. 5, no. 4, p. 629–643, August 1993.

[SHY 98] SHYU M.-L., CHEN S.-C., KASHYAP R.L., "Information Retrieval Using Markov Model Mediators in Multimedia Database Systems", *1998 International Symposium on Multimedia Information Processing*, p. 237–242, December 14–16, 1998.

[SIS 99a] SISTA S., KASHYAP R.L., "Bayesian Estimation for Multiscale Image Segmentation", *IEEE Int'l Conf. on Acoustics, Speech, and Signal Processing*, Phoenix, Arizona, March 1999.

[SIS 99b] SISTA S., KASHYAP R.L., "Unsupervised Video Segmentation and Object Tracking", in *IEEE Int'l Conf. on Image Processing*, 1999.

[SMO 94] SMOLIAR S.W., ZHANG HJ. "Content-based Video Indexing and Retrieval", *IEEE Multimedia*, p. 62–72, Summer, 1994.

[WOO 70] WOODS W., "Transition Network Grammars for Natural Language Analysis", *Comm. of the ACM*, 13, October 1970, p. 591–602.

[YEO 97] YEO B.-L., YEUNG M.M., "Retrieving and Visualization Video", *Comm. of the ACM*, vol. 40, no. 12, December 1997, p. 43–52.

[YEU 95] YEUNG M.M., LIU B., "Efficient Matching and Clustering of Video Shots", in *IEEE International Conference on Image Processing*, vol. I, October 1995, p. 338–341.

Chapter 2

Automatic video scene segmentation based on spatial-temporal clues and rhythm

Walid Mahdi and Liming Chen
Département MI, Laboratoire ICTT, Ecole Centrale de Lyon, France

Mohsen Ardebilian
Laboratoire HEUDIASYC CNRS/UTC, Compiègne, France

1. Introduction

With ever increasing computing power and data storage capacity, the potential for large digital video libraries is growing rapidly. These libraries will have thousands of hours of video, which will be made available, via the wide area networks, to users upon request [FAU 96, SMI 95].

However, the massive use of video for the moment is limited by its opaque characteristics. Indeed, a user who has to handle and retrieve sequentially needs too much time in order to find out segments of interest within a video. Therefore, providing an environment both convenient and efficient for video storing and retrieval, especially for content-based searching as this exists in traditional text-based database systems, has been the focus of recent and important efforts of a large research community [ARD 99, ARU 95, MAH 00].

The video coding scheme defined by MPEG-4 and the future MPEG-7 standards [MPE 99] offers several content-based functionalities, demanding a new organization of the video for better content description and understanding. Indeed, in order to enable content-based access of digital video libraries, the semantic and temporal structure embedded within a video must first be segmented, then indexed and searched with satisfactory recall and precision.

The majority of the existing automatic content-based segmentation of video consists of splitting the video into shots which are separated by cuts, and their detection is based on objective visual primitives such as color [SWA 91], image correlation, or 3-D hints [BER 89, ARD 00]. The shot represents the fundamental unit of manipulation of the video. So, by detecting the shot boundaries, it is possible to create indexes and to develop users' browsing tools enabling navigation and searching.

Unfortunately, the representation by shots of a video document does not describe its narrative and visual content well. Indeed, in such a case, the results of a user's query to a video library are a set of non-continuous time shots. They do not describe the narrative content of the video. Moreover, browsing thousands of shots contained in a video document (3225 shots in *October* of S.M. Eisenstein [AUM 94], 500 to 1000 shots in a normal film [AIG 94]), presents a great challenge for the user *during* his linear navigation and search for any particular video segment. Also the granularity of the information content is such that a one half-hour video may have ten semantically separate units, to each of which corresponds a scenario of the story board of the film.

Many approaches are proposed to improve search and navigation in the video medium. Their main idea consists in partitioning video data into small clips of meaningful data. A manual segmentation into 1600 video clips of a 45-hour library is considered by the Informedia Project [CHR 97]. Mills imposes a fixed segmentation into clips on the video data [MIL 92]. Ramin Zabih et al. describe in [RAM 95] an approach to the detection and classification of scene breaks in video sequences. Another a priori model has been proposed in [ZHA 94] for news broadcasts to extract certain specialized semantic elements of the video sequences. In our previous work, we proposed a method to detect strict alternate shots which are then combined into scenes [FAU 96].

In this paper, we propose a new automatic video scene segmentation method that explores two main video features; these are spatial-temporal relationship and rhythm of shots. The experimental evidence we obtained from a 80 minute-video showed that our prototype provides very high accuracy for video segmentation.

The rest of the paper is organized as follows. In Section 2, we briefly review related works in the literature, emphasizing strengths and drawbacks of each technique. In Section 3, we first define the problem by describing the video structure, we then present the general principle of our scene segmentation approach. Section 4 summarizes the 3-D hints-based algorithm used in our experimentation for video shot segmentation and parameterization. In Section 5, we introduce the clustering of video shots based on visual contents. Section 6 addresses the video scenes segmentation method based on spatial-temporal clues. A formulation of rhythm effect for video scenes segmentation is presented in Section 7. In Section 8, we detail our video scene segmentation method which couples the exploration of spatial-temporal relationships with the consideration of the rhythm effect. The experimental results that we have driven on a 80 minute-video selected from the movies *Dances With Wolves*, *Conte de Printemps* and *Un Indien dans la Ville* are then presented in Section 9. Further work is depicted in the last section.

2. Related work

While there is a lot of work reported in the literature focusing on shot boundary detection [AIG 95, ARD 00, CHA 94], there is, on the other hand, little work on the video scene segmentation. The first approach proposed the scene break detection on the basis of the image intensity signal analysis of the video stream. For instance, Otsuji and Tonomura [OTS 94] discuss a variety of measures based on the difference and change of intensity histograms of successive images. Nagasaka and Tanaka [AKI 94] present an algorithm using similar measures. Ramin, Miller and Mai propose a method in [RAM 95] based on the detection of intensity edges that are distant from edges in the previous frames. The limitation of this method appears clearly in the case where the video produces a rapid frequency of brightness changes which occurs for the total duration of the scene. In summary, the limit of these techniques is that they are only based on the spatial indication of the video stream and do not take into account the video temporal clues. Indeed, the global visual contents of successive images are not enough to differentiate different contexts. For instance, in the case of 'busy' scenes, the intensities may change substantially from frame to frame. This change often results from abrupt motion and leads to falsification of the scene break detection for these techniques based on similarity measures.

Jain Hampapur and Weymouth proposed another method [JAI 88], called *chromatic scaling*, which attempts to detect a variety of scene breaks based on an explicit model of the video production process. Their method implies the definition of a specific model for each type of video being analyzed. A particularly interesting approach is introduced by M. Yeung and Yeo [MIN 96, MIN 97]. For the first time they propose video shots clustering based on both visual similarities and temporal localities of the shots which they call *time-constrained clustering*. The

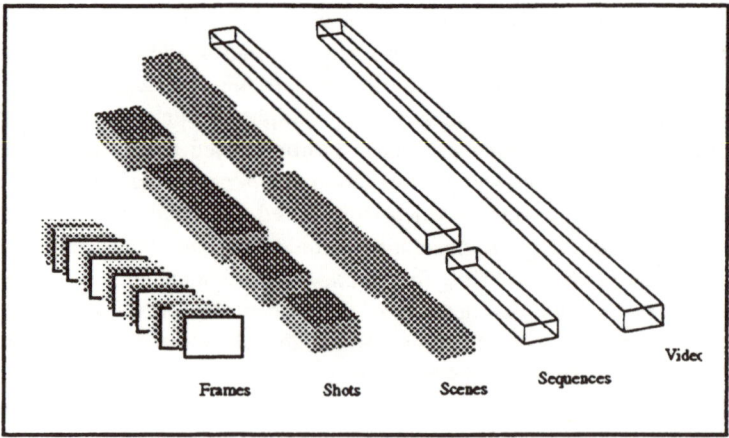

Figure 1. Video structure

goal of this method is to build a scene transition graph which provides the basis on which analysis can be performed to extract semantic story units. Unfortunately, the temporal locality criterion used in this method is difficult to generalize. Indeed, the choice of the temporal threshold, which imposes every scene to take place for a given time duration does not correspond to any video production rule. In our approach, we do not need such a temporal threshold. Instead, we use cinematic production rules to achieve scene break detection.

3. Video parsing: problem and principle

In this section, we first describe the semantic structure embedded within the video in order to clearly state the problem, then we introduce the principle of automatic scene segmentation within the framework based on spatial-temporal clues and rhythm.

3.1. Video structure

A video program such as motion pictures, TV movies, etc., has a story structure and organization. As illustrated in Figure 1, three levels define this syntactic and semantic story structure: narrative sequence, scene and camera shot. A camera shot is a set of *continuous frames representing a continuous action in time or space*. It represents the fundamental unit of production of video, reflecting a basic fragment of story units. A scene is a dramatic unit composed of a single or several shots. It usually takes place in a continuous time period, in the same setting, and involves the same characters. At a higher level, we have the narrative sequence, which is a dramatic unit composed of several scenes all linked together by their emotional and narrative momentum [AUM 94]. During the montage, which *refers to the editing of the film, the cutting and piecing together of an exposed film in a manner that best conveys the intent of the work*, two narrative sequences are linked together by an effect of transition such as dissolving or fading and two shots are linked by cuts. Consequently, this *temporal delimitation of sequences* criterion must be integrated in any model of video stream segmentation into semantic units.

To convey parallel events in a scene, shots of the same person or same settings, taken from the same camera, at the same location, are repeated, alternated or interleaved by other shots with different contents. Most often, the similarities of contents are shown through similar visual characteristics of the composition of frames in the shots.

Video is also characterized by a rhythm. In fact, certain editors produce rhythmical effects by using the duration of successive or alternative shots. Shots belonging to the same scene generally have the same or close rhythm. Moreover, shots which do not respect the current rhythm frequently carry out a scene break [AUM 94].

For automatic video parsing purposes, we first introduce an intermediate level of *clusters*, resulting in a *scene*, then a *sequence* which provides narrative unity as follows.

Definition 1 – Cluster

A cluster is a set of similar plans situated in a limited period of time.

Similarity generally implies a similar set having the same spatial distribution. For example, let Γ be the corpus of a film segmented into a set of shots Ω. Consider 5 consecutive shots in Ω: $p(k)$, $p(k+1)$, $p(k+2)$, $p(k+3)$, $p(k+4)$. If $p(k)$, $p(k+2)$ and $p(k+3)$ describe such a similarity on set, actors, etc., while $p(k+1)$ and $p(k+4)$ describe another similarity, then two clusters $\phi(i)=\{p(k), p(k+2), p(k+3)\}$, and $\phi(i+1)=\{p(k+1), p(k+4)\}$ are formed.

Based on this definition, we can define more precisely the notions of scene and sequence.

Definition 2 – Scene

A scene is a semantic unity formed by a set of successive shots temporarily continuous, sharing generally the same objects and/or describing the same subject.

Let $\phi(i)=\{p(k), p(k+2), p(k+3)\}$ and $\phi(i+1)=\{p(k+1), p(k+4)\}$ be two clusters sharing the same subject such as a telephone conversation and for which there exists no transition effect, then a scene $S(j)=\{p(k), p(k+1), p(k+2), p(k+3), p(k+4)\}$ is formed by the combination of $\phi(i)$, and $\phi(i+1)$.

Temporal continuance is defined by a non-interruption of the temporal projection of elements (shots) of this continuation (neither a plan miss nor an effect of transition exists between two consecutive plans). In other words, a scene is a semantic unity formed by a combination of additional clusters.

Definition 3 – Sequence

A sequence is a narrative unity formed with one or several scenes.

3.2. Principle

According to our approach, the video scene segmentation process consists of 3 steps: shot segmentation and parameterization, video shot clustering, and scene extraction. Figure 2 illustrates such a general process.

The shot segmentation decomposes the video into basic shots by detecting shot transition effect. Now there exists a lot of methods in the literature [ARD 00, RAM 95] for video shot segmentation. In this paper we suppose that shots and shot transition effects of a video are already segmented and are the input of our study. In our experience, we applied a 3-D hints-based method that we previously proposed [ARD 00]. A summary of this technique is presented in Section 4.

Video shots clustering aims at characterizing the spatial-temporal relationships between shots, and results in a set of clusters and a *temporal clusters graph (TCG)* capturing the temporal relationship between clusters.

Finally, we proceed to the scene segmentation. We first explore the *TCG* in order to get a rough scene segmentation. This result is then improved by the consideration of rhythm to obtain the final scene segmentation.

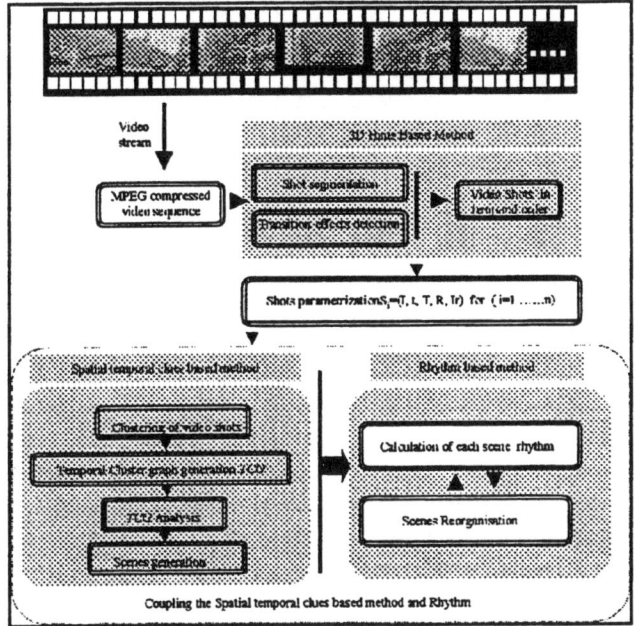

Figure 2. *The block diagram of proposed approach for video scene segmentation*

4. Video shots segmentation and parameterization

The understanding of image content using 3-D clues has been the focus of many researchers working in the image-processing field [MAG 96, QUA 88, ZHA 94]. Not only can such knowledge contribute to information compression, eventually leading to video compression, but also to classify the type of the scenes with their 3-D structures [AUM 94, CHE 94]. In this section, we briefly describe our method of video shot splitting by the use of the *focus of expansion (FOE)* in 3-D scenes. According to our method, we first realize linear contour detection. Then by the principle of duality which exists in projective geometry, we localize the FOE within an image by a *Double Hough Transformation (DHT)*. Finally, with the help of FOE position change in the video stream, we split the video into shots. It should be noted that color information is not used in our technique, because it may alter the method robustness when sudden illumination or color changes occur in the video.

Focus of expansion (FOE) can be used to derive 3-D structure information such as parallelism, orthogonality of line features. Quantitative analysis of FOE gives information about motion as well. After double HT, we obtain for each input image a pattern of discrete points (possible FOE points). The positions of these points are used as indices of shot segmentation of the video sequence. In two-point patterns derived from two successive images, we have developed a matching algorithm for calculating the global match between two discrete point patterns. The main purpose is to find a maximum resemblance pattern. Here is the algorithm of the discrete point comparison:

1. Choose between two patterns the one with the lowest number (n) of points.
2. Superpose two patterns and do iteration on the points for i=1 to n.
3. Calculate the maximum resemblance of a pair of points in a fixed sized zone; if no corresponding point is found, assign a penalty value.
4. Go to step 2 to continue for all pairs of points.
5. Calculate the global resemblance of two patterns by summing all local values normalized by n.
6. By the help of the shot transition models take a decision if there is a shot transition in the video sequence or not and identify its type (cut, dissolve, etc).

This algorithm is very fast for a direct comparison between two patterns. We have also tested the algorithm by dynamic programming, and graph matching with its node representing the points and the links representing the relation among the points. However, to be efficient, the algorithm above must be carefully tuned to the global threshold value for shot cut detection, as with the majority of all other shot detection techniques.

5. Clustering of video shots

In order to organize the video data as semantic units, we first characterize the spatial-temporal relationship within the video by clustering similar shots. Recall that a cluster of shots gathers a set of similar shots and represents a fragment of semantic units. Thus two shots are clustered together if the distance of dissimilarity between them is less than a predefined threshold.

5.1. Similarity of images

Similarity measures based on visual variables such as color, image correlation, optic flow, 3-D images, etc., can distinguish different shots to a significant degree, even when operated on much more compressed images such as DC images. We adapt the histogram intersection method from Swain and Ballard [SWA 91] to measure the similarity of two images based on color histograms. A color histogram of an image is obtained by dividing a color spectrum (e.g. RGB) into discrete image colors (called *bins*) and counting the number of times each discrete color appears by traversing every pixel in the image. Given two images Ii and Ij, and their histograms Hi and Hj, each containing n bins, we denote by $Hi(k)$ the value of Hi in the kth bin, the intersection of the histograms is defined as:

$$\sum_{k=1}^{n} \min\left(H_i(k), H_j(k)\right) \qquad [1]$$

This gives an indication of the number of pixels that have similar colors in both images. It can be normalized to match a value between 0 and 1 by the following formula:

$$S(H_i, H_j) = \frac{\sum_{k=1}^{n} \min\left(H_i(k), H_j(k)\right)}{\sum_{k=1}^{n} H_j(k)} \qquad [2]$$

For our purpose, we use mismatch value, calculated from equation (3), to indicate dissimilarity between the two images instead of the match value defined above.

$$D(H_i, H_j) = 1 - S(H_i, H_j) \qquad [3]$$

5.2. Temporal-delimitation for clustering of video shots

The clustering of video shots is aimed at grouping shots having similar content. For this purpose, we use the spatial-visual similarity combined with a temporal delimitation. Indeed, because of the temporal locality of the contents, if two similar visual shots occur far apart in the time line, they tend to represent different content or locale in different scenes. Each cluster of shots must be then in the same sequence to maintain semantic clustering. Generally, a sequence as described in [AUM 94], is linked to another one by an effect of transition (dissolve, fade-in or fade-out) to tell the spectator that a break in the narration of the history has occurred. Thus the process of clustering has only to be applied to each sequence separately. When all shots of a sequence are clustered a clustering of new sequence shots is brought out.

For the purpose of clustering, we assume that the shots and their parameters (t: time code, Td: time duration, R: representative image, R: effect of transition) of a video are already detected by means of the 3-D hints-based method. We also define $L(Si)$ a function which returns the transition effect R used to link shot Si with the shot $Si+1$. Our strategy of clustering consists of initializing a new cluster ϕk to the first shot Si which is not yet classified, then it compares this one (ϕk) to each successive shot $Sj(j>i)$ that is in the same sequence ($L(Si) \notin \{$dissolve, fade-in, fade-out$\}$). If they are similar ($D(Si, Sj) < T$ (threshold)), Sj is classified into ϕk. If not, the process of comparison is continued to the end of the sequence. When all shots of a sequence are clustered a new clustering of a sequence's shot is brought out.

5.3. Time-space graph generation

In order to organize the video data as a semantic unit, a new representation of the video data as a *time-space graph (TSG)* is then produced. The time-space graph is created as a new description model of the video stream. The TSG construction is based on shot boundaries detection and video shots clustering strategy as presented in the previous section. The vertical axis represents the spatial distribution of shots, the position of the cameramen or the clusters, with the horizontal representing the time line or the time code. Figure 3 illustrates a form of TSG, where τ is the time duration of an effect of transition between two sequences, t_i is the time code of the shot P_i and ϕ_i is a cluster that regroups some shots.

6. Video scenes extraction

Once we obtain the video clusters and characterize their temporal relationships, a new representation of the video stream, called *temporal-clusters graph (TCG)*, is built to carry out such temporal relationships between clusters. In contrast with the scene transition graph generated by M. Yeung and Yeo [MIN 96], the *TCG* generation is based on temporal presentation of multimedia programs. Video scenes are then extracted by analysis of temporal relationships on the TCG. For temporal presentation of multimedia programs, *Timing Petri-net graphs* [BUC 93] or *Allen temporal operators* [ALL 83] may be used. Timing petri-net is often used to obtain the expression of the synchronization of several multimedia objects such as audio stream and video stream within a video program. But the temporal modeling in such a graph may be complex for a long video program. In our work, as we only focus on the video stream, Allen operators are preferred because they offer the same expression power with greater simplicity.

6.1. Temporal-clusters graph generation

Based on TSG, temporal relationships between clusters are defined and captured by a temporal cluster graph TCG. To describe such temporal relationships between clusters, some new annotations are introduced for primitive temporal relations defined by Allen and described in [ALL 83]. In such a *TCG*, a node is associated with each cluster, and an edge is drawn for each temporal relationship

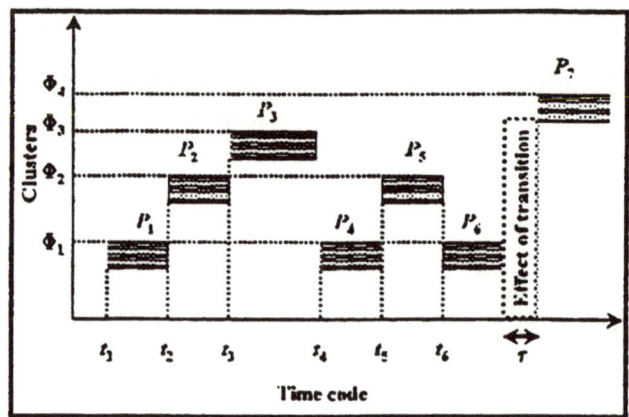

Figure 3. *Description of video data as TSG graph*

between two clusters. Figure 4 illustrates an example of TCG. This representation defines a video as a *directed acyclic graph* [LAY 96] where edges are time constraints on the duration as defined in Table 1. These time constraints give the allowable duration of intervals which is specified by the parameters of temporal relation. We also make use of two abstract time-nodes, *Begin* and *End*, corresponding to the time of the beginning and the end of a given video program. The *Begin* node is connected to all time-nodes which do not have incoming edges by means of special edges labeled with a particular delay. Similarly, all the time nodes which have no outgoing edges are connected to the *End* time node. This DAG representation of a video is used as the basis for the time constraints analysis. Figure 5 shows an example of a DAG corresponding to our previous example presented in Figure 4.

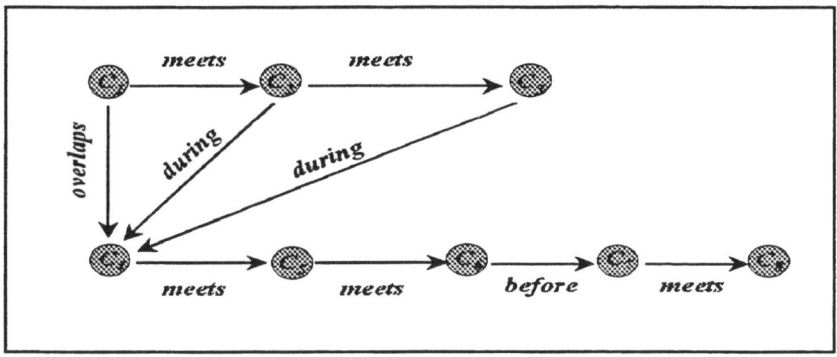

Figure 4. *An example of TCG graph*

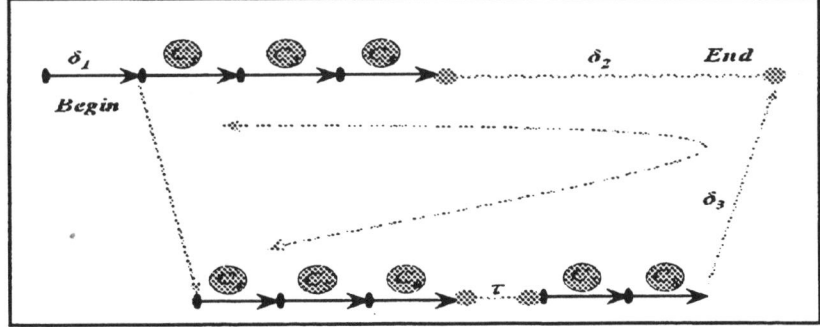

Figure 5. *Temporal Directed Acyclic Graph generated from the TCG*

Table 1. *Temporal relation's constraints*

Temporal relations	Temporal constraints
$\Phi_1 \, Meets \, \Phi_2$	$P_n^1.t + P_n^1.Td = P_1^2.t - 1$
$\Phi_1 \, Before \, (\tau) \, \Phi_2$	$P_n^1.t + P_n^1.Td + \tau = P_1^2.t - 1$
$\Phi_2 During \, (P_1^2.t,...,P_i^2.t,...P_{i+1}.t) \, \Phi_1$	$P_n^1.t + P_1^1.Td \leq P_i^2.t - 1 \, \&\& $ $P_i^1.t + P_i^1.Td \geq P_n^2.t - 1$
$\Phi_1 Overlaps \, (P_1^2.t,...,P_i^2.t,...P_{i+1}.t) \, \Phi_2$	$P_1^1.t + P_1^1.Td \leq P_1^2.t - 1 \, \&\& $ $P_n^1.t + P_n^1.Td \geq P_i^2.t - 1 \, \&\& $ $P_n^1.t + P_n^1.Td \leq P_{i+1}^2.t$

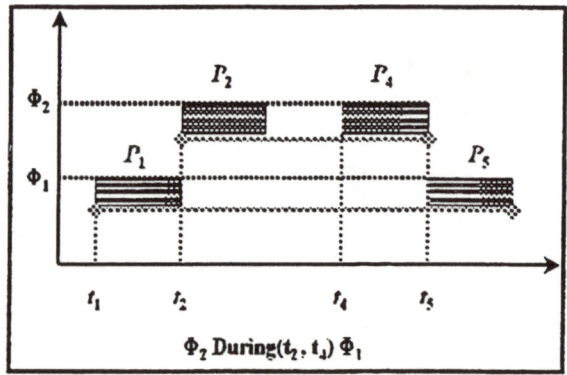

Figure 6. *During relationship generated from the TSG graph*

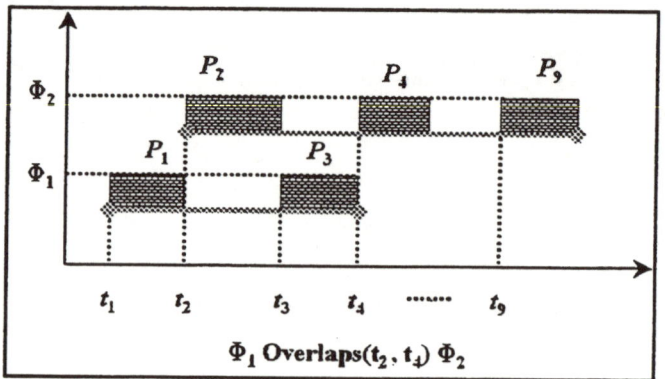

Figure 7. *Overlaps relationship generated from the TSG graph*

Given an arbitrary DAG representation extracted from the temporal cluster graph, the following properties can be stated:

- Certain routes are not allowed (Acyclic Graph) because *instants coming from the past can not be equal to instants in the future* and vice versa.
- Cycles are always composed of two parallel chains (*DAG property*) [LAY 96], whose total duration must be compatible. This property ensures that the two paths can be guaranteed at run-time, as illustrated in Figure 5.

Currently, we used four types of relations between clusters: *Meets, Before, During* and *Overlaps*. The first two describe a sequential relationship between two clusters. Therefore, they have only one parameter that represents the delay τ of succession between them. The *Meets* relation is generated between two clusters that are included in the same sequence, and no delay separates these two clusters. The *Before* relation describes a transition of sequences. Each member of this relation is included in a different sequence, then in a different semantic unit. The delay parameter represents the time duration of the effect of transition that links the two sequences together. *During* and *Overlaps* are used when two clusters intersect in time, as illustrated in Figure 6 and Figure 7. They indicate that their members are included in the same semantic unit. The time code of all shots of the left cluster of a *During* relation defines its parameters. For an *Overlaps* relation, its parameters are defined by the time code of all shots of its right-hand member in intersection with its left-hand member. In addition, the last parameter of this relation is the time code of the first shot of the right-hand member which is not in intersection with the left-hand member as illustrated in Figure 7. The succession and the intersection between two members of a temporal relation are determined by the space-time distribution of their shots. As a consequence of the previous definitions, these annotated temporal relations define a set of temporal constraints which must be satisfied. Table 1 summarizes all of these temporal constraints associated with the temporal relations. In the table, t represents the time code of a shot, Td the time duration of a shot and τ the time duration of the effect of montage that links one shot to its successor (if *cut* then $\tau = 0$ otherwise $\tau \neq 0$).

For the extraction of scene units, we first analyze the TCG according to the semantic of the temporal relationship between cluster nodes, leading to a first scene segmentation result. This result is then improved by the consideration of the rhythm effect to obtain the final scene segmentation.

6.2. Temporal-clusters graph analysis

Extracting semantic units of a video document consists of analyzing the four types of temporal relationships captured by a TCG: *Before, Meets, Overlaps* and *During*. Each one corresponds to some rule in the video production. We first describe these semantic correspondences:

- *Meets*: this separates two clusters which belong to two successive scenes.

These scenes belong to the same sequence. For instance, consider two shots *a* and *b* that belong to two different and successive scenes. Suppose that according to the shots clustering method as presented in the previous section, these two shots are classified in two different clusters. However, if the effect of montage that links shot *a* to shot *b* has a time duration equal to 0, a *Meet* temporal relationship is generated in order to separate two successive scenes.

    – *Before*: this separates two clusters that belong to two scenes of two successive sequences. This relationship occurs between two successive clusters when a montage feature is used, such as fade, dissolve, or using a time duration different from zero.

    – *Overlaps* and *During*: these describe a change in the temporal distribution of shots belonging to the same scenes. In other words, this type of relationship corresponds to the case where movie editors interleave, by means of a montage, several shots in order to describe a scene which takes place with a different setting but having a common subject. A classic example of using an *Overlaps* relationship is the telephone conversation.

We turn to the video segmentation process based on spatial-temporal relationships. Following from the previous analysis, we can see that the *Before* relationship divides a video into several sequences, and is used to separate a TCG into several independent subgraphs, called *sequence subgraphs*.

    Figure 4 illustrates a TCG which is split into two subgraphs by the *Before* relationship between clusters 6 and 7. Consequently, the semantic scene units must be separately searched in each *sequence subgraph* of TCG. For this purpose, the *Meets* relationship is used to divide each sequence subgraph into scene units, Γ, which are in their turn subgraphs of the sequence subgraph. Each subgraph Γ contains at least one shot. A series of successive shots obtained by the combination of all nodes of subgraph Γ describes the boundaries and the content of a semantic scene unit. The application of this process leads to a first scene segmentation result. We experimented with this process on a 45 minute-video from the movie *Dances With Wolves*, 15 minutes from the movie *Conte de Printemps*, and 20 minutes from the movie *Un Indien dans la Ville*. The experimental results are presented in Tables 5, 6, 7 and 8 of Section 9. As we can see from these tables, this process, which reaches a high success segmentation rate, has also the drawback of producing independent scenes formed only by one shot. This situation corresponds to a distortion of the real semantic of the video. This consideration leads us to apply an additional tool based on the rhythm which allows capture of the complete semantic embedded within a video.

7. The use of rhythm

Rhythm is a temporal effect that editors produce by using the duration of successive shots, leading to particular visual effects for each scene. For instance, a sunset scene in a video has a different rhythm as compared to that of an air-raid scene. Furthermore, the rhythm change between scenes is often dependent on the movement within scenes. Our previous example illustrates this fact. Sun in a sunset scene moves more slowly than two aircraft of an air-raid scene.

To explore the rhythm effect within a video stream, we first propose a statistical measure to detect the change or maintenance of the rhythm. We then discuss how such a measure can be used for our scene segmentation purpose.

7.1. Statistical characterization of rhythm

Experimental results show that shot duration in video can not be determined in advance and variation of shot duration follows a random distribution. Thus we may approximate a set of shot duration variations as a set of statistical variables. In order to describe the distribution of a statistical variable, we rely on a theoretical distribution which characterizes such a statistical variable according to a law of parametric probability.

The law of parametric probability which any statistical variable obeys is generally deduced from theoretical considerations and hypothesis. In our case, with the aim to study the distribution law of the variation of the duration of different shots within a same scene, we represent the whole set of these variation points on the plan (v, f), where v stands for the variation of the duration of shots, whilst f stands for the frequency of each variation. Figure 8 shows the histograms which correspond to different scenes extracted from several films. We can notice from the figure that the different histogram curves match a well-known distribution rule which has the shape of a bell. This rule is called in statistics the

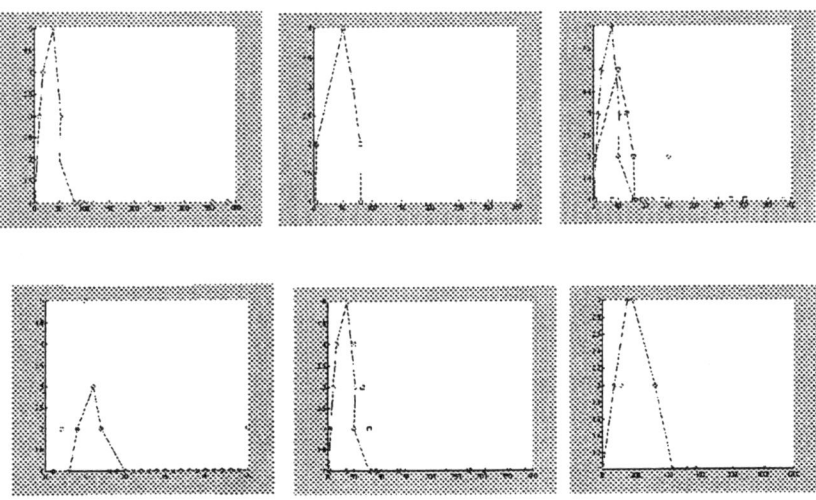

Figure 8. *Shot duration variation distribution; **a, b** and **c** three scenes from the film Dances with Wolves, **c** and **d** two scenes from the film Conte de Printemps, **e** and f two scenes from the sitcoms provided by INA*

normal law of distribution [SAB 93]. However, stating from a sample of videos that the variation of duration of shots in every film follows the normal law of distribution may lead to some error. Consequently, we make our assessment in a so-called *safe interval* which guaranties to a certain degree, that a point can be applied to a population of a statistical variable. In our case, we mean by population of a statistical variable a succession of video shots, and by *safe interval* the interval which statistically characterizes the two ends of a semantic scene.

7.2 Scene segmentation by the use of rhythm

Assume there exist N shots in a video $\varphi = \{P_1, P_2, \ldots, P_i, P_{i+1}, \ldots P_N\}$. Every shot P_i $(1 \leq i \leq N)$ is characterized by its time duration Td_i and its time code (starting time) t_i. Assume also that $VTPi, i+1$ is the duration's variation between shots P_i and P_{i+1}, that is $VTP_{i,i+1} = \mid P_i - P_{i+1} \mid$. Thus, to the set of shots φ, we associate a set of duration variations between each couple of successive shots P_i and P_{i+1} (with $P_i, P_{i+1} \in \varphi$).

Let $GP = \{ P_1, P_2, \ldots, P_n\}$ be a set formed by the first n $(n>2)$ and successive shots.

Let $GVTP = \{VTP_{1,2} \ldots VTP_n-1, n\}$. We define $F(GP)$ and $L(GP)$ as two functions which respectively give the first and the last shot belonging to GP. A new shot P_i $(n+1 \leq i \leq N)$ is considered to have the same rhythm as compared to shots in GP and is added to GP if it satisfies the two following conditions:

(a) The temporal continuity condition:
The insertion of the shot P_i to GP must ensure a temporal-continuity between shots P_j $(P_j \in GP)$, that is : $P_i t + 1 = PF (GP).t$ or $P_i t = PL (GP).t + 1$. This condition simply states that shot Pi must be the one which precedes the first shot or follows the last shot of GP.

(b) The aggregation condition based on the rhythm:

$$\mid VTP_{F(GP), i} - VTPM \mid \leq \alpha * \delta \quad \text{or} \quad \mid VTP_{L(GP), i} - VTPM \mid \leq \alpha * \delta$$

where:

– $VTPM$ is the average variation of the $GVTP$ set, and is calculated by equation 4.

$$VTPM = \frac{\sum_{i=1}^{n-1} VTP_{i,i+1}}{n} \qquad [4]$$

– δ is the standard deviation of the set $GVTP$, and is calculated by equation 5.

$$\delta = \sqrt{\frac{\sum^{n-1}_{i} \left(VTP_{i,i+1} - VTPM\right)^2}{n}} \qquad [5]$$

– α is a coefficient that determines the *safe interval* $I = [VTPM - \alpha\delta, VTPM+\alpha\delta]$.

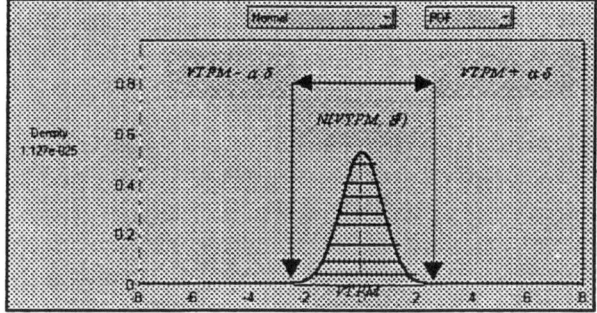

Figure 9. *The curve of a Normal Law density function*

Suppose that the set *GVTP* of rhythm changes is characterized by the curve of a normal low-density function as illustrated in Figure 9. If α is fixed to be value 2.5, and if the addition of a shot P_i, to the set *GVTP* leads to a new value of *VTPM* contained in *I*, then according to statistics theory, shot P_i will have a probability of 98% of being an element of the scene *GP*. When one of the two previous conditions is not satisfied, a new set *GP* is initialized with *n* (*n*>2) successive shots, and the process of shot grouping is tried again with the rest of shots still untreated. Generally, the value n is chosen according to the synoptic character that the segmentation process has to respect. This value generally depends on the type of video program. For instance, a *TV* news frequently comes back to the anchor person after a report which may be only composed of two shots. In this case, it would be necessary to choose for *n* a value corresponding to the minimum number of shots that a scene may have.

In our experience we have fixed *n* = 3 because of the synoptic character of the dramatic films on which we have conducted our experimentation. However, we rarely base our scene segmentation process just on the rhythm rule as we first use spatial-temporal clues which lead to an initial semantic shot aggregation, and thus the set of *GP* already formed. The following section explains how we couple the rhythm with spatial-temporal clues to more precisely capture temporal structure within a scene and between scenes in a video, to give the final scene segmentation.

8. Coupling the use of rhythm with spatial-temporal clues-based segmentation

Our segmentation process based on spatial-temporal clues [MAH 98], when applied to several samples of videos may lead to the creation of a so-called shot scene which is a scene formed by one shot. This is often a distortion of the semantic. Rhythm is used here to tackle this problem. Indeed, each shot scene is studied on the basis of rhythm in order to possibly be associated with the scene which immediately precedes or follows it. This coupling-based segmentation is achieved as follows:

- First, we apply the spatial-temporal clues-based segmentation to the video stream in order to obtain an initial result of scene segmentation.
  - Let $\Gamma = \{S_1, S_2...S_N\}$ be the set of scenes containing more than one shot.
  - Let $\chi = \{P_i,...P_j\}$ be the set of one shot scenes. Thus, $\forall P_i \in \chi$, and we have $\neg \exists S_i \in \Gamma$ such $P_i \in S_i$.

- Now each S_i in Γ is considered as a set of shots GP_i as already defined in the previous section. Notice that we do not have to choose a particular value for n and obtain a GP set already computed. We depict the informal algorithm as follows:

Input: Scenes $S_1...S_n$ already obtained by the spatial-temporal clues-based segmentation.

Step 0: Initially, there are n set of scenes $GP_1 \leftarrow S_1$; ...; $GP_n \leftarrow S_n$;

Step 1: Let χ_r, be the set of one shot scenes; $\chi_r \leftarrow \{\}$;

$// \chi_i$ contains the previous state of χ_i //

Step 2:

If $(\chi_r \neq \{\})$ //there is any one shot scene ?//

    2.0. $\chi_i \leftarrow \chi_r$;

    2.1. Select scene GP_i formed by one shot from χ_r;

    2.2. Look in Γ for all scenes GP_k which immediately precede or follow the one shot scene GP_i, i.e. $P_i. t = P_{F(GPk)}.t - l$ or $GPi. t = P_{\mu(GPk)}.t + l$;

    Else// there is no one shot scene//

    2.3. Go to **step 5**;

  Endif;

Step 3:

For each GP_k which has been chosen at **step 2.2**

    compute the set $GVTP_k$;

    compute $VTPM_k$;

    compute δ_k;

    //check the aggregation condition//

    If $(\mid VTP_{L(GPk)}._i - VTPM_k \mid < \alpha * \delta_k)$ or $(\mid VTP_{F(GPk)}.i - VTPM_k \mid < \alpha * \delta_k)$

      If $(GP_k$ corresponds to the scene that best matches the rhythm)

      $GP_k = GP_k + \{GP_i\}$;

      // the one shot scene is removed from the set χ_r //

      $\chi_r = \chi_r - \{GP_i\}$;

      Endif;

    Endif;

  Endif;

End;

Step 4:

If $(\chi_r \neq (\chi_i)$ // is there any aggregation ?// go to **step 2**; **Endif**

Step 5: Stop.
Output: scenes $S_1...S_p$ with $p \leq n$

Once the above algorithm is applied, there may be some groups of successive shots which remain and do not belong to any segment. They are then handled as follows:

– In case a group of successive shot scenes is formed by more than two shots *(n>2)*, the rhythm-based scene segmentation technique that we have introduced in Section 7 is applied to obtain a synoptic segmentation.

– Otherwise each shot scene is considered as a scene which is often used in order to emphasize a jump in the narration or a jump in the film time.

9. Experimental results

In order to show the efficiency of our coupling model for the semantic scene segmentation purpose, we have implemented a prototype in *Matlab* and *Visual C++* using the standard collections *STL* on a *Pentium-II* based machine. We have driven experiences on segments extracted from three movies: 15 minutes of *Conte de Printemps*, 20 minutes of *Un Indien dans la Ville*, and 45 minutes of *Dances with Wolves* with Kevin Costner. They have been chosen for the variety of style. All the sequences are compressed in MPEG-1. In our experiences, all MPEG sequences were first decoded and segmented into parameterized shots by the 3-D hints-based method [ARD 00]. These parameterized shots are then used as an input to our study. Each shot is represented by a key frame at a spatial resolution of 288×352 with each pixel coded by 32 bits (16M colors). A summary of the shot segmentation results is shown in Table 2. We can see in Table 2 that the first segment of the movie *Dances with Wolves* contains two dissolves detected at frame 70 and frame 98, which can be used as temporal delimitation for the scene segmentation. For the other segments, there is no transition effect, thus in this case only the rhythm is used for the temporal delimitation. Table 3 provides the scene segmentation results by three methods: spatial-temporal clues-based method, coupling method and expert-based manual segmentation. Column 4 in this table shows the number of clusters obtained by the clustering process. Recall that our clustering process is based on histogram color comparison and uses the measure of dissimilarity with the threshold $T = 0.1$. Figure 10 shows the result of clustering

Table 2. *Results of 3-D hints-based method for shot segmentation and parameterization*

Type	Sequence Name	# Shots	# Dissolves
Movie segment	*Conte de printemps*	67	0
Movie segment	*Un indien dans la ville*	85	0
Movie segment (1)	*Dances with wolves*	130	2
Movie segment (2)	*Dances with wolves*	150	0

Table 3. Results of sample test sequences

Sequence Name	# Shots	# Frames	# Clusters	# Story units(1)	# Story units(2)	# Story units(3)
Conte de printemps	67	13820	46	25	5	4
Un indien dans la ville	85	24120	63	32	6	5
Dances with wolves (1)	130	34020	69	23	10	8
Dances with wolves (2)	150	37500	99	5	4	3

(1): Story units segmented by the spatial-temporal clues-based methods.
(2): Story units obtained by the spatial-temporal clues-based methods coupled with rhythm
(3): Story units identified by an expert.

Table 4. Content of clusters

Cluster	Frame numbers
C16	*16*
C17	*17*
C18	*18*
C19	*19, 24*
C20	*20, 23*
C21	*21, 22*

after 15-minutes in *Conte de Printemps*. Table 4 shows the content of some clusters which result from the clustering process shown in Table 3.

These are used to generate the TCG, illustrated by Figure 11, which characterize the temporal relationships among clusters of the video. Story units (scenes) can be extracted by analyzing these temporal relationships as explained in Section 6.2. In Figure 11, we have a part of the TCG on the 15 minutes *Conte de Printemps* which describes the temporal relationships among clusters *16, 17, 18, 19, 20, 21* and *22* highlighted in Figure 10. Each edge in the graph in Figure 11 represents a temporal relationship between two clusters. Generally there may be four types of temporal relationship which are *Overlaps, During, Before* or *Meets*. We can observe in Figure 11 two temporal relationship types, *During* and *Meet*, describing the following relations:

1. *C16 Meets C17*
2. *C17 Meets C18*
3. *C18 Meets C19*
4. *C19 Meets C22*
5. *C20 During (19, 22) C19*
6. *C21 During (20, 21) C19*
7. *C21 During (20, 21) C20*

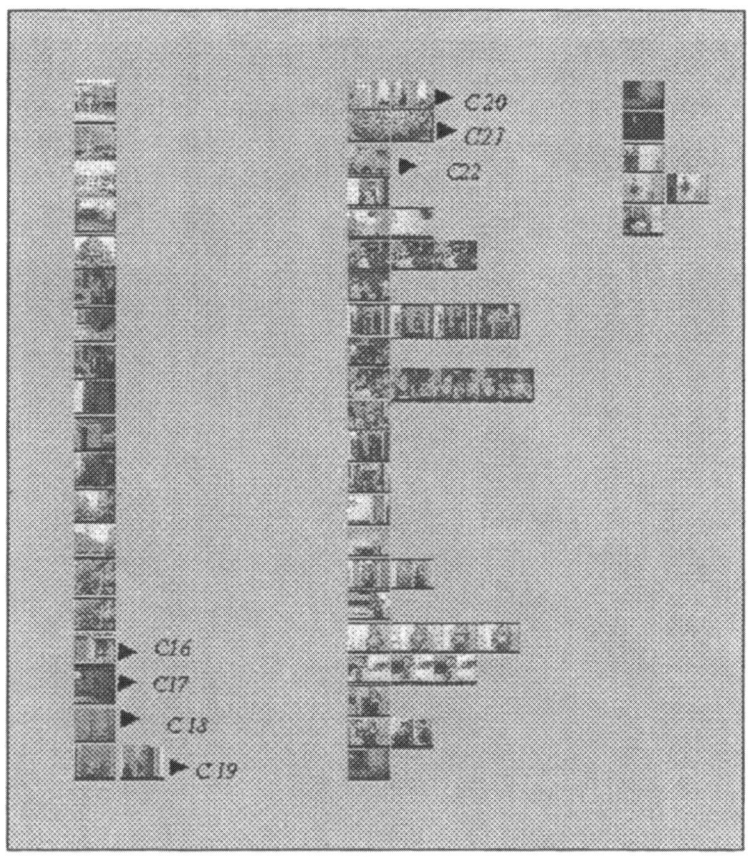

Figure 10. *Clusters obtained after the clustering process on 15-minutes Conte de Printemps*

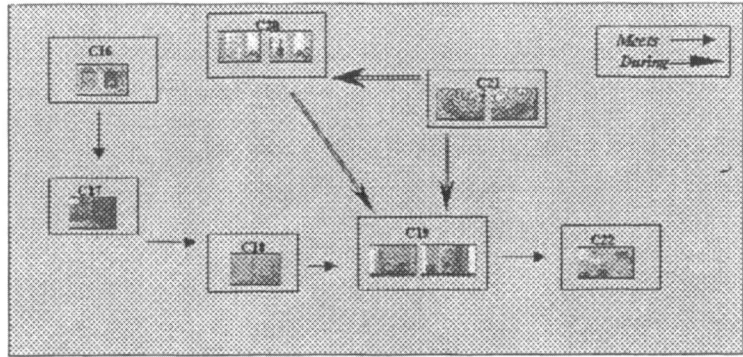

Figure 11. *A sample of the TCG built on the 15-minutes Conte de Printemps*

As described in Section 6.2, the *During* relationship characterizes a change in the temporal distribution of shots belonging to the same scene. Therefore, clusters *C19*, *C20* and *C21* are merged into one scene. On the other hand, if we only rely on spatial-temporal relationships for the scene segmentation, we know that the *Meets* relationship occurs when two successive clusters belong to two different successive scenes. Thus clusters *C16, C17, C18,* and *C22* would each generate a scene. However, when looking into the video, an expert-based manual segmentation would gather *C16, C17* and *C18* into one scene with the one formed by *C19, C20* and *C21* because of their intrinsic semantic showing that one lady goes back to her home. Similarly for cluster *C22*. Fortunately, as illustrated in Figure 12, the analysis of rhythm gives other information which eventually leads to merger on one hand *C22*, and on the other hand clusters *C16, C17* and *C18* with the scene formed by clusters *C19, C20* and *C21*. As we can see in the figure, cluster *C22* is first merged into the scene (*C19, C20, C21*), then *C18, C17* and finally *C16*. Table 3 summarizes the scene segmentation results using three different methods. While column #7 gives the number of scenes resulting from an expert-based manual segmentation, columns #5 and #6 respectively give the results using the spatial-temporal clue-based segmentation method and the coupling segmentation-based

Table 5. *Experimental results on the 20-minutes Un Indien dans la Ville*

Spatial temporal clue based segmentation method			Coupling method			Expert results		
N° Scene	Begin	End	N° Scene	Begin	End	N° Scene	Begin	End
1	Shot 19	Shot 24	1	Shot 1	Shot 14	1	Shot 1	Shot 14
2	Shot 29	Shot 44	2	Shot 15	Shot 25	2	Shot 15	Shot 26
3	Shot 45	Shot 66	3	Shot 27	Shot 44	3	Shot 27	Shot 44
Remaining Shots considered as scenes			4	Shot 45	Shot 66	4	Shot 45	Shot 66
1, 2, 3, 4,…18, 25, 26, 27, 28			Remaining Shots considered as scenes			Remaining Shots considered as scenes		
				26			-------------------------	

Table 6. *Experimental results on the 15-minutes Conte de Printemps*

Spatial temporal clue based segmentation method			Coupling method			Expert results		
N° Scene	Begin	End	N° Scene	Begin	End	N° Scene	Begin	End
1	Shot 6	Shot 12	1	Shot 1	Shot 5	1	Shot 1	Shot 5
2	Shot 24	Shot 56	2	Shot 6	Shot 16	2	Shot 6	Shot 17
3	Shot 57	Shot 65	3	Shot 18	Shot 56	3	Shot 18	Shot 56
4	Shot 66	Shot 73	4	Shot 57	Shot 65	4	Shot 57	Shot 65
Remaining Shots considered as scenes			5	Shot 66	Shot 85	5	Shot 66	Shot 85
1, 2, 3, … 5, 13, 14,..,23, 74, 75, …,85			Remaining Shots considered as scenes			Remaining Shots considered as scenes		
				17			-------------------------	

Table 7. *Experimental results on the 20-minutes Dances with Wolves (CD-1)*

Spatial temporal clue based segmentation method			Coupling method			Expert results		
N° Scene	Begin	End	N° Scene	Begin	End	N° Scene	Begin	End
1	Shot 1	Shot 29	1	Shot 1	Shot 29	1	Shot 1	Shot 29
2	Shot 33	Shot 47	2	Shot 31	Shot 51	2	Shot 31	Shot 50
3	Shot 53	Shot 66	3	Shot 53	Shot 66	3	Shot 51	Shot 65
4	Shot 71	Shot 97	4	Shot 67	Shot 70	4	Shot 66	Shot 70
5	Shot 101	Shot 116	5	Shot 71	Shot 98	5	Shot 71	Shot 98
6	Shot 117	Shot 128	6	Shot 100	Shot 116	6	Shot 99	Shot 116
Remaining Shots considered as scenes			7	Shot 117	Shot 130	7	Shot 117	Shot 130
30, 31, 32, 48, 49, 50, 51, 52, 67, 68, 69, 70, 98, 99, 100, 129, 130			Remaining Shots considered as scenes			Remaining Shots considered as scenes		
			30, 52 and 99			30		

Table 8. *Experimental results on the 25-minutes Dances with Wolves (CD-2)*

Spatial temporal clue based segmentation method			Coupling method			Expert results		
N° Scene	Begin	End	N° Scene	Begin	End	N° Scene	Begin	End
1	Shot 2	Shot 25	1	Shot 2	Shot 25	1	Shot 1	Shot 25
2	Shot 26	Shot 63	2	Shot 26	Shot 64	2	Shot 26	Shot 64
3	Shot 65	Shot 150	3	Shot 65	Shot 150	3	Shot 65	Shot 150
Remaining Shots considered as scenes			Remaining Shots considered as scenes			Remaining Shots considered as scenes		
1 and 64			1			-------------------		

method where we have fixed $T = 0.1$ and $\alpha = 2.25$. Tables 5, 6, 7 and 8 detail the scene segmentation results on the three movies, giving the content of each segmented scene by the three methods. As we can see in the tables, while the spatial-temporal relationship based segmentation method provides good results, it also produces many one-shot scenes. The use of the rhythm removes this drawback, leading to fully successful scene segmentation as compared to the expert manual segmentation.

10. Conclusions and future work

We propose a new scene segmentation method, which couples the exploration of spatial-temporal relationships with the consideration of video stream rhythm. Our method, applied to a video, automatically decomposes the video into a hierarchy of scenes, clusters of similar shots and shots at the lowest level. Experience on a 80-minute video stream extracted from the movies *Dances with Wolves*, *Conte de Printemps* and *Un Indien dans la Ville* shows our method produces a very high scene segmentation success rate as compared with expert manual segmentation.

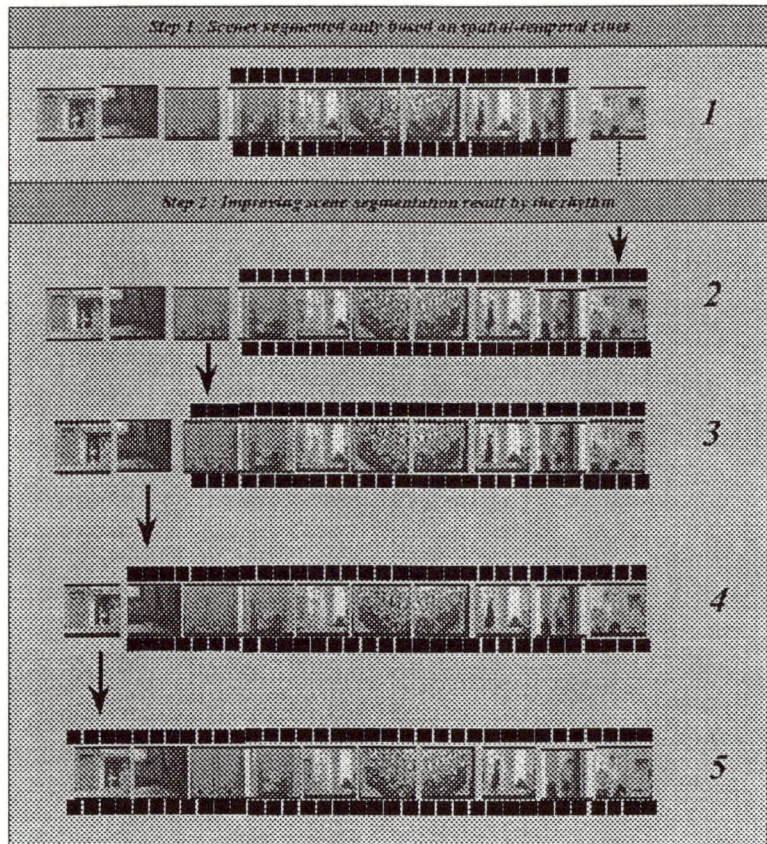

Figure 12. *Use of rhythm for rectifying the drawbacks of one shot scenes produced by the spatial-temporal clues-based segmentation*

Our future work includes the exploration of other spatial clues, for 2-D and 3-D impressions, for a better shot clustering, and definition of techniques for further video macro-segmentation based on sequence segmentation.

Recently, we have worked out two new techniques for the segmentation of other significant clues, that is image classification into *inside/outside* and *day/night* images, and the localization of texts embedded within a video program. Based on these techniques, we have been extending our scene segmentation work on other video materials such as commercials and TV news.

REFERENCES

[AIG 94] AIGRAIN P., JOLY P., "The Automatic Real-time Analysis of Film Editing and Transition Effects and its Application". *Computer Graphics* 18 (1), pages 93–103, 1994.

[AIG 95] AIGRAIN P., JOLY P., LOUGUEVILLE V., "Medium Knowledge-based Macro-Segmentation of Video into Sequences". *IJACI Workshop on intelligent Multimedia Information Retrieval*. ED. Mark Maybury, Montreal, 1995.

[AKI 94] AKIO N., AND TANAKA. Y., "Automatic Video Indexing and Full-video Search for Object Appearances". In *2nd Working Conference on Visual Database Systems*, October 1994.

[ALL 83] ALLEN J.F., "Maintaining Knowledge about Temporal Intervals". *CACM,* 1983, Vol. 26, pages 832–843.

[ARD 99] ARDEBILIAN M., MAHDI W., CHEN L., "Exterior and Interior Shots Classification for Automatic Content-based Video Indexing". *Proceedings SPIE, Conference on Multimedia Storage and Archiving System IV*. Vol. 3846, pages 46–55, USA, Boston. 20–22 September 1999.

[ARD 00] ARDEBILIAN M., CHEN L., TU X.W., "Robust Smart 3-D Clues Based Video Segmentation for Video Indexing". In the *Journal of Visual Communication and Image Representation*, March 2000, Vol 11, N°1, pages 58–79.

[ARU 95] ARUN H., RAMESH J., AND WEYMOUTH T., "Production Model Based Digital Video Segmentation". *Journal of Multimedia Tools and Application*, 1:1–38, March 1995.

[AUM 94] AUMONT J., BERGALA A., MARIE M., VERNET M., *"l'Analyse des films"*. Nathan editor (1994), ISBN 2–09–180–711–9 Chap. 2.

[BER 89] BERGEVIN R., LEVINE M.D., "Generic Object Recognition: Building Coarse 3D Descriptions from Line Drawings", *Proceedings of IEEE Computer Society Workshop on Interpretation of 3D Scenes*, November 27–29, Austin, Texas, pages 68–74, 1989.

[BUC 93] BUCHANAN M.C., ZELLWEGER P.T., "Automatic Temporal Layout Mechanisms", *Proceedings of the First ACM International Conference on Multimedia*, pages 341–350, Anaheim, California, August 1993.

[CHA 94] CHANDLER D., "The Grammar of Television and Film". UWA, 1994, ([und]*http://www.aber.ac.uk/~dgc/gramtv.html*[undx]).

[CHE 94] CHEN H., LIN W.C., LIAO H.Y.M., "Recovery of Superquadric Primitive from Stereo Images". *Image and Vision Computing*, vol. 12, N° 5, pages 285–295, 1994.

[CHR 97] CHRISTEL M.G., WINKLER D.B., AND TAYLOR C.R., "Improving Access to a Digital Video Library". *In Human-Computer Interaction: INTERACT97, the 6th IFIP Conference on Human-Computer Interaction*, Sydney, Australia, July 14–18, 1997.

[FAU 96] FAUDEMAY P., CHEN L., MONTACIÉ C., X.W. TU, CARATY M.J., FERNANDEZ C., AND ARDEBILIAN M., "Multichannel Video Segmentation", *Proceedings SPIE, Conference on Multimedia Storage and Archiving Systems I*, Boston, pages 252–264, November 1996.

[JAI 88] Jain A.K., and Dubes R.C., *"Algorithms for Clustering Data"*. Prentice Hall, 1988.

[LAY 96] Layaïida N., "Issues in Temporal Representations of Multimedia Documents". *Workshop on Real Time Multimedia and the Web 96, World Wide Web Consortium*, INRIA, Sophia-Antipolis, October 1996.

[MAG 96] Magee M.J., Kaggarwal J., "Determining Vashing Points from Perspective Images", *Computer Vision Graphics and Image Processing 26*, pages 256–267, 1996.

[MAH 98] Mahdi W., Liming C., Fontaine D., "Improving the Spatial Temporal Clue Based Segmentation by the use of Rhythm", *2nd European Conference on Research and Advanced Technology for Digital Libraries (ECDL '98)*, Heraklion, Crete, Greece, 21–23 September 1998, in LNCS 1513, ISBN.3–540–65101–2, Springer, Editor. C. Nikolaou, C. Stephanidis, pages 169–182.

[MAH 00] Mahdi W., Ardebilian M., Chen L., "Automatic Scene Segmentation Based on Exterior and Interior Shots Classification for Video Browsing". *IS&T/SPIE's 12th Intl. Symposium on Electronic Imaging 2000, Proceedings SPIE*. San Jose, California, USA. Vol. 3974. 26–28 January 2000.

[MIL 92] Mills M., Cohen J., Wong Y.Y., "A Magnifier Tool for Video Data". *Proceedings of CHI '92*, pages 93–98, May 1992.

[MIN 96] Minerva M. Yeng, Boon-Lock Yeo, "Time-constrained Clustering for Segmentation of Video into Story Units", In *Proceedings of ICPR*, pages 375–380 1996, IEEE Press.

[MIN 97] Minerva M. Yeng, Boon-Lock Yeo, Wayne Wol and Bede Liu, "Video Browsing using Clustering and Scene Transition Compressed Sequences", In *Proceedings of Multimedia Computing and Networking, Proceedings SPIE,* Vol. 2417, pages 399–413, San Jose, California, USA.

[MPE 99] *"MPEG7 Standard"*, [und]*http://drogo.cselt.it/mpeg/standards/mpeg-7/mpeg-7.html*[undx].

[OTS 94] Otsuji K., and Tonomura Y., "Projection-detecting Filter for Video Cut Detection". In *Multimedia Systems 1*, pages 205–210, 1994.

[QUA 88] Quan L., Mohr R., "Matching Perspective Images using Geometric Constraints and Perceptual Grouping", *Proceedings ICCV*, Florida, pages 679–683, 1988.

[RAM 95] Ramin Z., Iustein M., Kevin M., "A Feature-Based Algorithm for Detecting and Classifying Scene Breaks", *Multimedia '95*, San Francisco, CA, USA, ACM, 1995.

[SAB 93] Sabin L.M., Statistique: Concepts et Méthode, Masson editor, 1993, chapter 6 pages 216. ISBN 2–225–84189–6.

[SMI 95] Smith M.A., and Kanada T., "Video Skimming for Quick Browsing Based on Audio and Image Characterization". *Technical Report CMU-CS-95–186*, 1995.

[SWA 91] Swain, M.J., and Ballard, D.H, "Color Indexing". *International Journal of Computer Vision*, Vol. 7, No. 1, 1991, pages 11–32.

[ZHA 94] Zhang H., Gong Y., and Smoliar S., "Automatic Parsing of News Video". *Proceedings of IEEE Conference on Multimedia Computing and Systems*, Boston, USA, 1994.

Chapter 3

Dynamic generation of video abstracts using an object-oriented video DBMS

Hervé Martin and Rafael Lozano

IMAG – Laboratoire Logiciels, Systèmes, Réseaux, St Martin d'Hères, France

1. Introduction

Video systems have received tremendous interest recently. The main reason is the ability of computing systems to support video data. For a long time, video data were managed by specific environments because their size and resource needs were not supported by computing systems. Improvements in data compression formats such as MPEG-4, networks transfer rates and operating systems [LAU 94] have opened new application areas. Many applications such as video on demand, video conferencing and home video editing are targeted by these systems.

Database management systems, like other systems, must be extended to support video data types and to propose more satisfactory solutions than 'binary large objects' (blobs). Nevertheless, the integration of video data in a DBMS framework entails several problems. Firstly, such data types must be physically managed apart from other conventional data types so as to fulfill performance requirements. Secondly, video modeling must be addressed according to the hierarchical structure of a video (shots, scenes and sequences) but also in a more general way in order to allow overlapping and disjointed segment clustering [WEI 95]. DBMS must provide a query language where queries may involve video data. This means that video query language must allow one to query video content using textual annotations or computed signatures as color, shape or texture. More specific features related to video such as those related to the movement of objects in the scenes would be also provided. Moreover, such a language must deal with semi-structural aspects of videos and must offer the capability of creating new videos.

This paper presents the approach proposed by the VStorm system and introduces the video abstract paradigm proposed in this context. The VStorm system [LOZ 98b, LOZ 00] allows capture of video data in an object DBMS and also to take advantage of database and object-oriented capabilities within a video context. Video DBMS offer various advantages such as data sharing, data consistency and data re-usability. Re-usability would be improved by providing a standard and flexible way to access data. Thus, the utilization of standardized query language such as OQL must be investigated. We proposed in [LOZ 98b] some extensions to OQL for querying video data.

The important feature of digital video DBMS is the capability of navigating across a large volume of data by avoiding linear video playback which takes a long time to visualize the entire video (despite facilities such as fast forward and fast backward). In this paper we explore new ways for optimizing the time for watching video. We introduce the paradigm of *dynamic abstract*. This paradigm aims to take into account the fact that depending on video content relevance and user feedback, the system may dynamically adapt video duration. Some works have been realized through video abstracts [DEM 98, LIE 97, MAY 97, SAA 99] to provide a way to statically reduce the initial length of video data. In this paper, we go further by allowing users to determine practically and dynamically the time they want to spend in watching video. When a relevant sequence is found the user has the possibility of exploring more accurately the video stream. We show how a video database system can implement this paradigm and we propose a graphical user interface to control time and video content during presentation.

The remaining parts of the paper are organized as follows. In the next section, we present the video model which represents the basis of other proposals. Section 3 introduces the video abstract paradigm. Section 4 describes the implementation that we realized; this realization uses the paradigm of abstract in order to control video duration during visualization. Finally, in the conclusion we provide some perspectives to this work.

2. Video model

This section summarizes the VStorm video data model. The VStorm video data model relies on different concepts which allow us to easily manipulate video data. Video data functionalities are enhanced when they are captured and organized in a database environment. In this section, we present our approach in order to (1) create and compose new videos from existing ones (2) specify relationships between video segments (3) annotate video segments.

2.1. Virtual video

We introduce the concept of virtual video in order to point out differences between the raw video stored in the database and the video which is watched and manipulated by end-users. This consideration is current in a DBMS framework [ANS 75]; [GAN 95] also proposes such an issue. From a user's point of view, a video is a continuous media which can be played, stopped, paused, etc. From a DBMS point of view, a video is a complex object composed of an ordered sequence of frames. Each frame is displayed for a fixed time (e.g. 1/30 sec.). Because the system distinguishes frames, it is possible to create new videos using frames from different videos (see Figure 1). In this example, a virtual video is specified using segments from two raw videos named RV1 and RV2.

For many applications, a video is made up from different video segments which may belong to various videos and because of the digital aspect of the video, it is possible to avoid replication. A virtual video covers various aspects. It can be a raw video, a part of a raw video, different segments from the same raw video or finally different segments of various raw videos. There is no constraint about the way of constructing virtual videos. A digital video editing system or other sophisticated tool (e.g. automatic extraction of relevant video streams) allows us to produce new virtual videos. In our object database context, the query language OQL (Object Query Language) [CAT 93] is used to extract video segments to be inserted in the video. The OQL query language does not provide any facilities to ask for specific features such as color, shape or movement. Such features are not treated in our approach. The only way to take those features into account is to straighforwardly annotate video with information related with this purpose. A virtual video is composed of video segments. Each video segment is specified using either directly a video interval (e.g. [lower–bound, upper–bound]) or a video query expression which is expressed using OQL plus extended functionalities. In Figure 2 is an example of four virtual videos (VVI, VV2, VV3 and VV4) specified from two raw videos (V1 and V2). It is very important to note that virtual videos VV3 and VV4 are defined over virtual videos VV1 and VV2. From the user's point of view, there is no difference between raw videos and virtual videos.

Video query expressions are stored in the database and the final video is generated at presentation time. This approach is close to the relational view concept and it avoids data replication. The query language OQL has functional aspects and allows the utilization of methods in queries. A video query expression returns:

– *A video interval* (video–name, frame–start, frame–end) which is a continuous sequence of frames belonging to the same video, either raw or virtual.

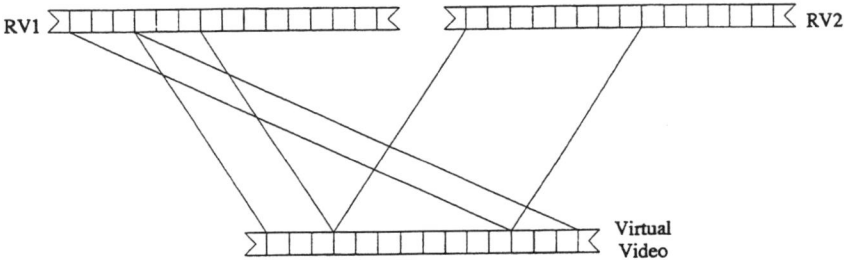

Figure 1. *A video stemming from two raw videos*

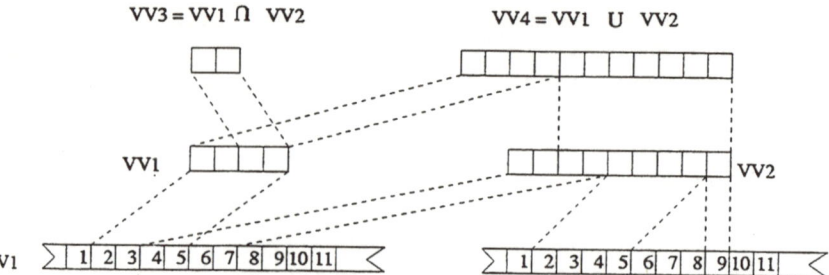

Figure 2. A virtual video creation example

VV1 = V1 – >extract(10, 500)

This expression shows that frames between 10 and 500 must be included into the virtual video VV1. Note that VV1 is a database object which refers to the excerpt.

– *A whole video*. A whole video could be retrieved according to properties such as attribute value.

```
VV2 = element(select V.Video
                from Video Database V
                where V.TITLE = "Dolce Vita" and
                     DIRECTOR = "Frederico Fellini")
```

In this example the 'Dolce Vita' video is retrieved and VV2 object references it. The method *play* may be applied to VV2 (VV2.play) for watching it.

– *An excerpt of a raw video* (this capability is a combination of the two former examples).

```
VV3 = element(select V– >extract(10,50)
                from VideoDatabase V
                where V.TITLE = "Dolce Vita" and
                     DIRECTOR = "Frederico Fellini")
```

– *A logical extract* of a video stemming from various raw videos. The following example creates a video composed of all video segments where 'Marcello Mastroianni' appears but not 'Anouk Aimee'.

```
VV4 = VUnion (select a.vi
                from Annotations a
                where 'Marcello Mastroianni' in a.keywords and
                     not ('Anouk Aimee' in a.keywords))
```

The VUnion operator avoids data duplication. The VV4 video object will be a list of references to video segments. In order to organize and filter the query result, some operators issued from the video algebra initially proposed in [OOM 93] and also used in [WEI 95, HJE 95] are defined. The algebraic operators are also used in order to express video composition.

Video composition is realized using a set of algebraic operators which permit the combination of video segments in different ways. The operators of video algebra are the following:

- Concatenation ($E1 \oplus E2$): this operation takes two videos ($E1$ and $E2$) and creates a new video composed of the first video followed by the second.
- Union ($E1 \cup E1$): this operation has the same features as the concatenation operation but common footage is not repeated.
- Intersection ($E1 \cap E2$): this operation creates a new video where only common footage of E2 and E1 is captured.
- Difference ($E1 - E2$): this operation creates a new video which is composed of the frames of the first operand without the common frames of the second operand.
- Ordered set ($!E1$): this operation drops redundancies in a video while keeping its order.

Compared with other works, we show how algebraic operators can be integrated into a query language.

2.2 Video semantic description

Videos contain semantics which must be represented and organized in order to really capture video in a database system. In this way each frame and segment of the video has a visual content which must be described and captured in a database structure. This description can be realized using manual, semi-automatic or automatic methods.

Automatic indexing of video data is still an open area of research [ZHA 93, AIG 94]. The term *annotation* is used to describe salient objects or events appearing in single video frames or into video segments. Each annotation is linked to a semantic unit and describes its meaning. The goal is to help users in his/her task of searching and retrieving video data. Annotations are structured in order to support queries. The OVID system [OOM 93] organizes annotations using hierarchical links. The AVIS [ADA 96] system is based on ER diagrams where entities are predefined. Such representations are not flexible enough to deal with various applications domains.

Our indexing mechanism is supported by an object database. In this framework, we have the opportunity to let the user decide the index structures. Any database object could refer to a video segment.

In practice, we adopted a manual indexing scheme supported by specific tools. The interface, shown in Figure 3, allows us to index videos by browsing video data and by associating keywords with specific video intervals. Then this information is stored in the multimedia database and can be updated and used for querying purposes.

Annotations are stored as database objects belonging to the class Annotation which can be refined according to application and user requirements. However, it

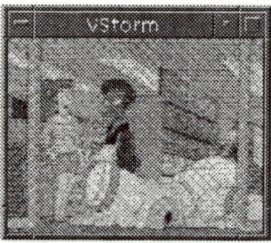

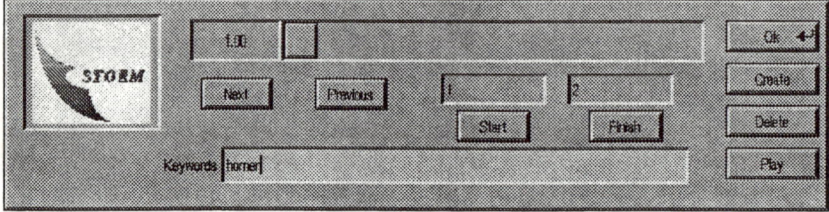

Figure 3. *Annotation tool*

supposes that the user who issues queries has a detailed knowledge of the database scheme. To avoid this, we proposed in [LOZ 98b] a video query language inspired by Generalized Path Expressions [CHR 94] in order to express fuzzy queries. For instance, the following query allows creation of a new video with all video segments where Anita Ekberg appears.

```
VV5 = VUnion(select 1
              from Videos V.intervals(I),
              AnnotationsA..#Attr(x)
              where x = "Anita Ekberg" and equal(A.interval,1)
```

This query searches any interval which can be reached from V and returns video intervals which get "Anita Ekberg" as an attribute value. This attribute must be reached from an annotation object (referenced by the A variable). The Attr attribute variable is instantiated during the query evaluation process with the name and the type of each attribute reached from an annotation object. Finally, *VUnion* operator eliminates redundancies.

Another important feature of video annotations is that they inherit the temporal characteristic of the video that they describe i.e., there is a temporal order between these annotations. This order can be, of course, used for query purposes and information can be inferred. Note that our proposal is very close to MPEG-7 [ORG 99, NAC 99] which also proposes a collection of classes in order to represent both metadata and low level features. Compared to our proposal, MPEG-7 provides a description data language but does not supply any way to exploit it (query language). Moreover, we propose an environment where it is possible to specify several indexing schemes in the same video database.

2.3 Multi-level video abstraction

The last point of the video data model concerns video composition which specifies relationships among video segments by defining a hierarchical view of the video. Many works have been initiated on this aspect from strict hierarchical structure [MON 81] to multi-straits modelling allowing overlapping, discontinuance and hyperlinks [JIA 98]. In these models, structure is inferred from annotations, therefore it is usual to observe overlapping and discontinuance. In the context of our model, the virtual video construction allows these capabilities and the annotation mechanism is orthogonal to the structuration mechanism. Thus, we keep a simple hierarchical structured model. Figure 5 shows the graphical interface offered to the user in order to construct a video and Figure 4 shows an example of a video with its hierarchical structure. While annotations are used for retrieving specific video data from a video database, hierarchical video structure is used to obtain the video context of a video segment. In this way we can show the result of a video query in a structured way. The following levels are specified:

– **frame:** the image which represents the smallest physical and logical unit. Note that from a semantic point of view, objects inside the image could also be considered (e.g. MPEG-7 standard) but they belong to another dimension of the video data model (Section 2.2).

– **shot:** a shot is a single camera action. Actually, several robust and efficient algorithms allow us to automatically detect shots inside a video. Shots are the basic building blocks of the hierarchical structure. Some algorithms based on pairwise comparison of pixels or pixel histograms comparison allow one to automatically detect shot boundaries [BOR 96].

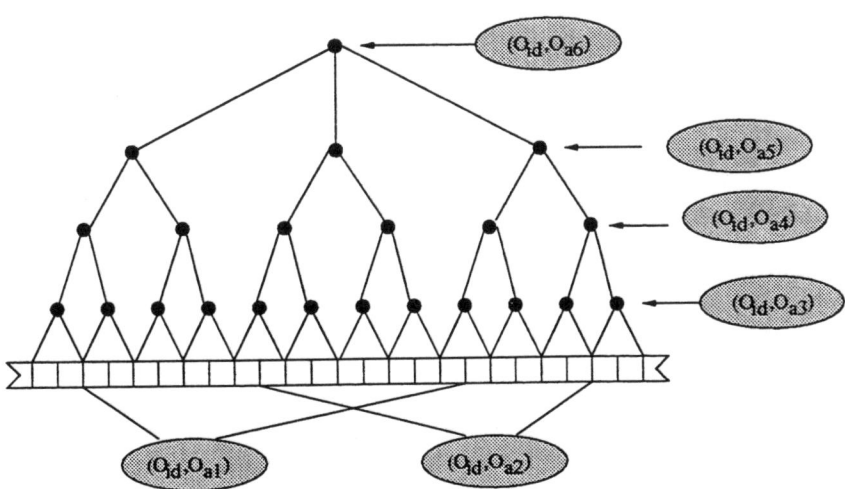

Figure 4. *Video hierarchical structure*

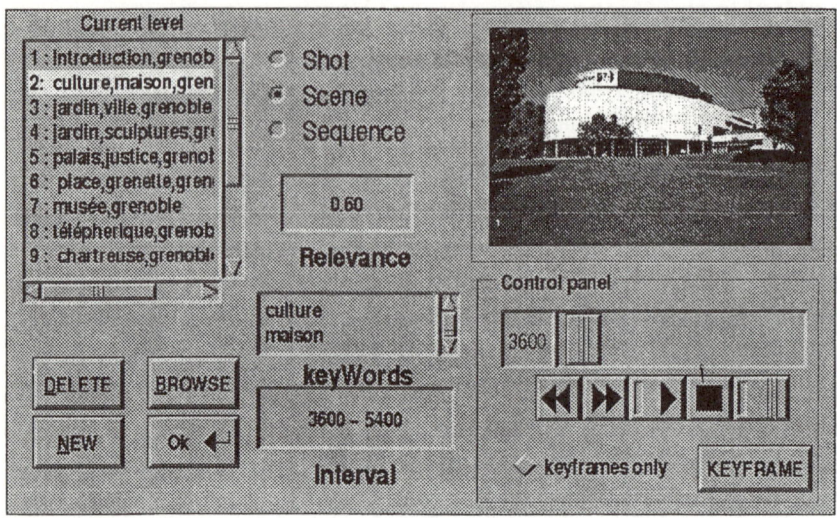

Figure 5. *Video segmentation*

– **scene:** a list of continuous shots having a unity of action and location. Scene and sequence change detection is more complex.

– **sequence:** a list of continuous scenes with a unity of action.

NOTE.—There is no correct way that levels of the hierarchical structure are defined and created. We just redefine them in order to facilitate the presentation of video abstract generation.

We adopted a bottom up approach to create the hierarchical structure of a video. It means that the shot level is defined before the scene level and so on. For each level in the hierarchy a member of a level must have one father and only one. It implies that there is neither overlap nor holes in the video structure. Figure 4 is an example of video hierarchical structure. NOTE.—There is no real limitation with this hypothesis. Video composition process is not limited by the way a video is structured. Therefore, it is possible to extract any video segment from a specific video without regarding its structure.

This description is stored as a metadata in the video database. We can use keywords, keyframes or in a general way a multimedia presentation as metadata in order to describe sequence, scene, shot or the whole video. The description process starts with the lowest level (i.e. the shot level). The description of a scene consists of the union of the descriptions of each shot which compose this scene but also the description of the meaning of this scene as a whole i.e. the reason for grouping the shots or the aggregate value of the set. This process continues until the top level of the hierarchy is attained. Video descriptions can be presented to the user using all the descriptions or only the aggregate value descriptions for a specific level.

Besides metadata which are used for description purposes, we define a factor (the relevance factor) which measures the contribution of each element of the hierarchical structure (e.g. a shot) to the global semantics of the group (e.g. a scene). Relevance factor is a way to measure the relative weight between the elements of the group. High values contribute more than low values.

Relevance factor is specified by a human being with its own objectivity. The principle is to specify the importance of each element according to others. The default value is adjusted in a way that all members of the same level which have the same father (i.e. belonging to the same group) also have the same weighting i.e. they have the same importance regardless of their duration. The sum of the relevance factors of all the members in the same level and with the same father must be 100%. The relevance factor plays a very important role in the generation of video abstracts (see Section 3).

Figure 5 shows the way that a hierarchical structure is created, more specifically the creation of scenes. Window "current level" shows all scenes which have been already created. In this way the same interface is used to create new members of the hierarchical structure but also for editing the members already created. Adding a new scene is a straightforward task. First of all, we have to select a scene radio button and use the "NEW" button to clear "keyWords" and the "Interval" windows. To capture the shot interval for this scene, we can use either the "Control panel" to watch the video or directly use the cardinal number of the first and last shot. The "Browse" button is used to link database objects with this scene. In this way not only a textual description is used for a member of the hierarchical structure but also objects of the database which could be more descriptive than words alone. *"KEYFRAME"* button is used to select the frame which is used to represent all the whole scene while the *"keyframes only"* button is used in each hierarchical level, to watch not all the video but its keyframes.

3. Video abstract

3.1. Objectives and approach

An abstract is a restricted view of a document that must include its most representative aspect and thus must therefore omit details. In the case of text media, it is possible to rewrite a document using the same language but with a different content. For video media, the task is more complicated because it is quite difficult to create a video with new content in terms of frames. Consequently, one must choose a subset of frames which is relevant to the video. Various features may be considered to determine the choice. Most of the existing works [LIE 97, DEM 98, MAY 97] try to reduce video duration either by random omission of frames or by selecting frames according to properties such as color and texture. We list below criteria which we consider in the context of our work.

  – The *part of the video to take into account.* Usually, the whole video is considered when computing its abstract. Because our video model is flexible in the sense that a video is virtual and can be composed of various segments of various videos, we enlarge this capability. An abstract summarizes a video, either real or virtual. As presented below, the query language OQL is used to determine the video part to be summarized. For instance the query "create an abstract with all video parts related to Fellini", is expressed by the following query:

```
VV6 = VUnion(
                select V.Video
                from Video Database V
                    where DIRECTOR = "Frederico Fellini")
```

Then, we apply the method *abstract*:

```
ABST1 = VV6–>Abstract(300)
```

ABST1 is a new video object with a duration of 300 seconds. This object may be played or re-used in a different context. Accuracy of each part may also be considered as in the framework of information retrieval.

– The *duration of the required abstract*. Saving user time is the main motivation of video abstract generation. The duration is measured in terms of time and thus in number of frames to select. The video abstract duration determines the content and not the opposite. This assumption is based on the objective that an abstract is user driven by time specification. In our proposal, we consider two parameters which are related to video abstract duration:

- The *duration established by the user*. In Section 4, we describe an interface which allows the users to control the duration (abstract last) of a video and to jump from one view to another (each view representing an abstract).
- The *video time minimal unit that is the smallest time for a video segment duration*. For instance, it makes no sense to create an abstract of two seconds because this duration is too small for user perception. Then, it is relevant for temporal media to let the user determine both the smallest time unit to consider as perceptive and also the granularity in terms of the structure of the result. For instance, it is possible to decide to create an abstract out of all scenes where a condition is satisfied. This means that for a given duration, the system must select the more relevant scenes. Works realized by [SAC 94] show that the minimum length for a continuous shot should be at least 3.5 seconds to be processed completely by the brain.

Note that duration may also be shortened using hard techniques such as the adjustment of transfer rates or the dropping of frames in a random fashion.

– *Information about content which is available*. This parameter is difficult to interpret and to address. Advanced algorithms on video content and captions are a way of capturing the semantics associated with the video. In our video system, while specifying video structure, it is possible to specify the relevance of each segment. The relevance is a real value which ranges from 0 to 1 and quantifies the semantic interest of a video segment.

– The *video structure*. This hierarchical structure provides a high level and sound view of the video. For instance, if a video is structured into twenty scenes it means that there are twenty different parts to summarize and this information is used to capture at least a piece of any scene whatever its duration. The video structure is also used to determine the granularity of the result. For instance, an abstract may group all relevant frames, scenes or sequences according to user requirements. Usual approaches just consider the frame levels. Nevertheless, in the same way that we have key frames, we propose to specify key scenes and key sequences. This task is performed using the relevance factors.

– *Abstract layout*. The definition of abstract must be considered in the perspective of a multimedia system and not only in the perspective of video systems. Such an environment allows support of the presentation of several videos in different ways. From a layout point of view, there are many possibilities: (1) present several videos in parallel (2) one frame per video (3) modify the order among segments. Thus, according to choice, it is possible to create several abstracts of the same video.

It is possible to play with different criteria and it is possible to obtain two abstracts of the same video of the same duration and different content.

3.2. Algorithm

From the analysis presented in the former section, we developed an algorithm which is based on this information. The algorithm is composed of four steps:

Step 1: *Retrieving all segments which could be selected to be part of the abstract.* Usually, this step is performed using a query expression or a graphical user interface such as the interface presented in the next section. The query expression is more powerful because it allows us for example to specify the granularity of the answer.

Step 2: *Associating any selected video segment with a value.* This value specifies a cosine which represents the distance between the set of keywords which annotate the segment and the set of keywords specified in the query. This method is a sample application of the method proposed by [VAN 79] in the vector model. It should be possible to take into account content signatures such as color or shape as proposed in QBIC [FLI 95].

Step 3: *Computing a general abstract factor.* This factor is a linear combination of three values:

  – The cosine formerly presented.
  – The relevance factor introduced in section 2.3 which is set by the video designer during the annotation process. It is dependent on the elements of the structure.
  – The relative duration of the segment which is computed according to the video structure. Normally, long segments are more relevant than

short ones. Each segment is compared to segments of the same level with the same father. For instance, we compare durations of all the scenes belonging to the same sequence.

In practice, we consider the same weighting for each value. Thus the linear combination consists of calculation of the average of these values and normalization with respect to its "brothers". Obviously, relevance factor and relative duration are correlated. It should be necessary to provide a graphical interface for tuning each factor in order to promote the user's wishes by increasing cosine weight or to promote intrinsic properties (relevance factor and relative duration). This capability has no deep effect on the algorithm. Such an operation is beyond the scope of this paper but is an interesting open issue for this work.

Step 4: Computing the final duration of each segment in the abstracting and organizing of all the segments in the abstract. At this level some segments may be dropped. The video abstract must preserve the video's structure and in particular the order among frames, while keeping the temporal balance among structure elements.

This process begins at the top level of the structure (using the duration established by the user) and continues until the last level of the hierarchy (i.e. the shot level). The next example shows how this operation is performed (each member of the hierarchical structure is represented as a tuple, *group([< first-element >, < last-element >], duration, relevance factor)*:

Shot level

$\{sh1([1, 1800], 1', 100\%), sh2([1801, 1'30'', 4500], 25\%), sh3([4501, 8100], 2', 50\%),$
$sh4([8101, 9900], 1', 25\%), sh5([9901, 15300], 3', 30\%), sh6([15301, 18000], 1'30'', 30\%),$
$sh7([18001, 22500], 2'30'', 40\%), sh8([22501, 24300], 1', 100\%),$
$sh9([24301, 27000], 1'30'', 75\%), sh10([27001, 29400], 1'20'', 25\%)\}$

Scene level

$\{sc1([1, 1], 1', 50\%), sc2([2, 4], 4'30'', 50\%), sc3([5, 7], 7', 100\%), sc4([8, 8], 1', 60\%),$
$sc5([9, 10], 2'50'', 40\%)\}$

Sequence level

$\{sq1([1, 2], 5'30'', 20\%), sq2([3, 3], 7', 60\%), sq3([4, 5], 3'50'', 20\%)\}$

Top level (Video)

$\{v([1, 3], 16'20'', 100\%)\}$

The following example is the generation of an abstract of 8' for this same video. The distribution of time among elements of the hierarchical structure is as follows:

$$\{abstract(v, 8')\}$$

Sequence level

$$\{sq1(1'36''), sq2(4'48''), sq3(1'36'')\}$$

Scene level

$$\{sc1(48''), sc2(48''), sc3(4'48''), sc4(58''), sc5(38'')\}$$

Shot level

$$\{sh1(48''), sh2(12''), sh3(24''), sh4(12''), sh5(1'26''), sh6(1'26''), sh7(1'56''),$$
$$sh8(58''), sh9(28''), sh10(10'')\}$$

In the first step, we infer the sequence duration from the video abstract duration. In the original video, there are three sequences whose relevance factors are respectively 20%, 60% and 20%. Consequently, we keep 20% of the time for the first sequence (that is 20% * 8 * 60" = 96 seconds or 1' 36"). In the same way, we apply the same process to each element of the hierarchical structure.

It is easy to transform time into frames (for videos whose play frequency is constant) to obtain the original video summary. However, at this point of the abstract generation some problems may occur.

The first one takes place when the time for a specific shot is so short we can not obtain enough frames to show something with meaning. Some studies show that the minimum length for a shot is 3.5 seconds. Below this the shot can not be processed by the human brain. In this case the time of the abstract for the element will be a little longer than the required time.

The second problem arises when there is not enough video information to satisfy the required time i.e. an abstract which is longer than the duration of the element! However this case could happen because of the way of calculating the abstract factor. An abstract of 10' for the same video will be like:

Top level (Video)

$$\{abstract(v, 10')\}$$

Sequence level

$$\{sq1(2'), sq2(6'), sq3(2')\}$$

Scene level

$$\{sc1(1'), sc2(1'), sc3(6'), sc4(1'12''), sc5(48'')\}$$

Shot level

$$\{sh1(1'), sh2(15''), sh3(30''), sh4(15''), sh5(1'48''), sh6(1'48''), sh7(2'24''),$$
$$sh8(1'12''), sh9(36''), sh10(12'')\}$$

Shot 6 and shot 8 present this kind of problem because their durations are respectively 1' 30" and 1'. The worst case happens when the user requests an abstract with the same (or almost the same) duration of the original video. To obtain the maximum time video abstract which can be obtained keeping the established abstract factor for each member, i.e. the relative proportions of the elements, we need to calculate, first, the Absolute Abstract Factor (*AAF*) for each member of the hierarchy. The *AAF* is the contribution, in percentage, that a member provides with respect to the whole video. The absolute factor of a member is the multiplication of its abstract factor by the asbtract factor of its father or group. In our example:

Top level (Video) 100%

Sequence level

$$\{sq1(20\%), sq2(60\%), sq3(20\%)\}$$

Scene level

$$\{sc1(10\%), sc2(10\%), sc3(60\%), sc4(12\%), sc5(8\%)\}$$

Shot level

$$\{sh1(10\%), sh2(2.5\%), sh3(5\%), sh4(2.5\%), sh5(18\%), sh6(18\%), sh7(24\%),$$
$$sh8(12\%), sh9(6\%), sh10(2\%)\}$$

The maximum time of an abstract keeping the abstract factor for each member is given by the following formula:

$$Max_{time}(Video_{abstract}) = Min_{time}\{shot_i \rightarrow duration/shot_i \rightarrow AAF)$$
$$\forall i \in \{shots\}\}$$

For our example:

$$Max_{time}(Video_{abstract}) = Min_{time}\{1'/10\%, 1'\,30''/2.5\%, 2'/5\%, 1'/2.5\%,$$
$$3'/18\%, 1'\,30''/18\%, 2'\,30''/24\%, 1'/12\%,$$
$$1'\,30''/6\%, 1'\,20''/2\%\}$$
$$= Min_{time}\{10', 60', 40', 40', 17', 8'\,20'', 10'\,25'', 8'\,20'',$$
$$25', 66'\,40''\}$$
$$= 8'\,20''$$

We can also define a factor which determines the absolute importance (in the whole video) for each member of the hierarchical structure. This factor is defined as:

AIF (**Absolute Importance Factor**) $= element \rightarrow AAF/element \rightarrow duration$

Elements with higher *AIF* are selected before elements with smaller ones. In other words, the system will show completely an element before another in a video abstract, if the first one has an *AIF* greater than the second one. We can use this factor to solve our previous problem i.e. when the time required for a specific element is greater than the duration of the element.

In this case the remaining time is distributed between the remaining elements (elements which are not completely filled) in such a way that the relative proportions between them are kept. The general algorithm to obtain a video abstract is as follows:

Algorithm to create a video abstract of $t_{abstract}$ seconds (for each element, T represents the time assigned to it in the abstract)

1) Sort the list of shots using the AIF in descending order

2) $current =$ first element of the list

3) $T = current \rightarrow AAF * t_{abstract}$

4) $If(T < current \rightarrow duration)$ go to 9

5) For the remaining elements, re-calculate in the following way:

$$element \rightarrow AAF = element \rightarrow AAF/(1 - current \rightarrow AAF)$$

6) $t_{abstract} = t_{abstract} + (T - current \rightarrow duartion)$

7) $current =$ next element of the list

8) $go\ to\ 3$

9) For the remaining list do:

$$T = current \rightarrow AAF * t_{abstract}$$

This algorithm proposes a way to generate a video abstract using a linear combination of three factors. One of these factors is set by the user using a query expression.

In a single video context, queries are used to "overload" the relevance factor established by an expert (see Section 2.3). This is not exactly an overloading because these factors are linearly combined to obtain the abstract factor but it tries to hide the relevance factor. Whereas, in a video collection context, it establishes the relative weights needed between elements (shots, scenes, sequences) which belong to different videos in order to be able to create a video abstract of the answer.

A video (or an element of its video structure) and a video query are represented by a vector in the same way as a text document. The dimension of the vectorial space which is used to represent the video is given by the number of different terms which are used to describe it i.e. the "vocabulary" used. In this way each different term is represented by a specific position in a vector and its value is directly proportional to its weight or importance to describe the element. After that, we use the dot product (scalar product) between two vectors to measure the similarity between two vectors and in this way be able to retrieve videos which are similar to the vector query. It means that at this step we mix all together the textual representation of video elements (annotation) and the video structure information. The objective is not to compare these representations but to take into account in a similar way both structure and content.

In this context, results of video queries are a list of ranked videos i.e. a list where the videos are listed in descending order of relevance. Relevance in this context is determined by the application of the measure of similarity. For instance, it is possible to create a video with an abstract of each video in the ranked list in such a way that videos which are higher ranked have proportionally higher duration than videos which are lower ranked. In this case a vector query is used to establish a relevance factor between videos which have not been related before.

Vector space model is also used to query single videos. In this case the idea is to retrieve video elements (e.g. scenes with a vector representation) which are similar to a video vector query. Again, the result of this query is a list of ranked scenes which are presented as a video abstract. A video abstract is generated using the user wishes (i.e. the element ranked list) but also the relevance factor established by the expert and the size factor (see Section 3.2 for details).

A drawback of this approach occurs when the ranked list is very long. In this case only videos that have a relevance higher than a specific limit will be selected for the generation of the video abstract.

After computing each element separately, we compute the video abstract. It means that previous criteria are merged. Obviously, the resulting abstract can be slightly different according to the importance the system decides to give to each criteria. By default, the importance of relevance is set to 2 and the importance of the structure is set to 1.

4. Abstract browsing system

Our abstract browsing system aims to dynamically generate video abstracts. We consider that the same video can be presented in different manners according to time specification.

All kinds of databases offer tools such as query languages to retrieve information. Query languages are widely used to request information in an "easy" and standard way. In multimedia databases, answers to multimedia queries can be very huge in data volume terms. Thus, a multimedia database must be concerned with both the query specification and also with the way that this answer can be manipulated. If a database is able to retrieve information which is 100% relevant to the user, the user has to spend a lot of time if he/she is looking for only a little segment of this information or he/she wants to spend only a few minutes (e.g. a video news) watching this media. A multimedia database must provide this kind of service.

Video abstract generation is our answer to this problem. The size of a video abstract is determined by the user and it corresponds to the time he/she wishes to spend watching the video. Using duration information, the video DBMS tries to generate a video with the best content. The problem is to translate "best" in a computational way.

In this section, we introduce two concepts for assisting the user in the task of quickly reaching relevant video segments. The first concept concerns the automatic creation of video abstract according to time specification and video segmentation. The second concept concerns navigation. We introduce a way for adapting the video content according to the video's structure and a way for navigating through the video's structure and its content. These capabilities are proposed using the graphical interface of Figure 6.

Video browsing and access have been widely discussed. For example [CHR 99] proposes a solution to create geographic references to video stored in a digital video library. They introduce the concept of map that shows the geographical entities addressed in a given stay. Another work [HOL 99] proposes a multimedia

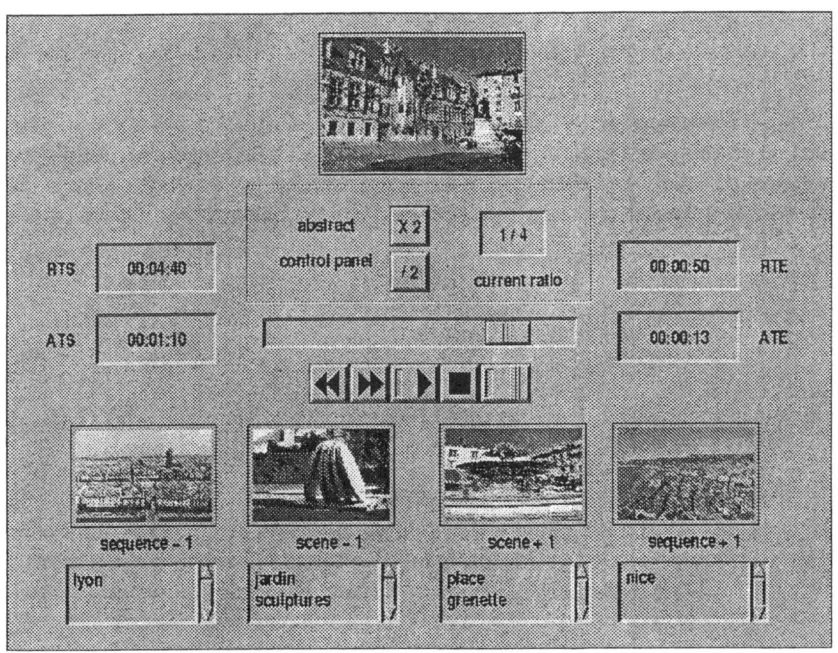

Figure 6. Elastic time and hyper link control panel

DBMS with a retrieval engine that calculates relevance values for the result of a conceptual query by feature aggregation on video shot granularity.

The top panel allows the user to control time before finishing the presentation. For instance, in this example, it waits 50 seconds until the end. It means that the user has decided to set the video presentation duration to 50 seconds. It is up to the system to propose the video content to display according to this time. The 'X 2' and '/2' items allow adjustment interactively of the remaining time of the video. The central left timer indicates the real time consumed from the video start. The timer at the right of the video indicates the real time until video end. Video actual duration is RTS + RTE. The control panel under the video proposes the usual VCR facilities and operates using a logical time scale. The lower part of the screen is dedicated to navigational aspects. The key frame of the previous and next scene and sequence is displayed with a corresponding keyword list. By clicking on such an image, the user activates an hypervideo link and accesses directly to the corresponding video part. Keywords and key frames related to video are displayed at the bottom of the control panel.

In addition to video hierarchical structure which allows dynamic building of the 'best of' all the possible video abstracts, navigation plays an important role. It allows jumping from one hierarchical element to another one in the same level (e.g. from one scene to another or from one sequence to the next sequence).

Each frame displayed to the user activates a video presentation, when the user clicks inside the frame. Links allow jumping from one member of the hierarchical structure to another one in the same way that we use the table of contents of an electronic book. Also it allows one to jump to the video segment where a keyword (e.g. a movie star) appears. As this is similar to the index table of an electronic book it can be implemented using indexes: a scene index table and a sequence index table. Each index associates any scene or sequence with pointers to the next and the previous scene and sequence.

This tool is just an example of a possible application of our proposal. The main idea that we developed is the fact that working with video structure, video content and content relevance it becomes possible to propose several views of the same video. Moreover, because of database content updates some queries will not produce necessarily the same abstract.

4.1. Implementation issues

A video is an object which covers several aspects: physical storage, logical structure and indexing. We consider different types of videos which are modeled using the class hierarchy of Figure 7. The root of this hierarchy is the VIDEO class which specifies generic operations such as play, pause or rewind. From a physical viewpoint, a video is a list of frames which must be played at a continuous rate (e.g. 30 frames per second). Raw video objects belong to the RAW–VIDEO subclass and capture the physical video data. Actually, we just consider the MPEG-2 format for video with associated management methods. Nevertheless, it is

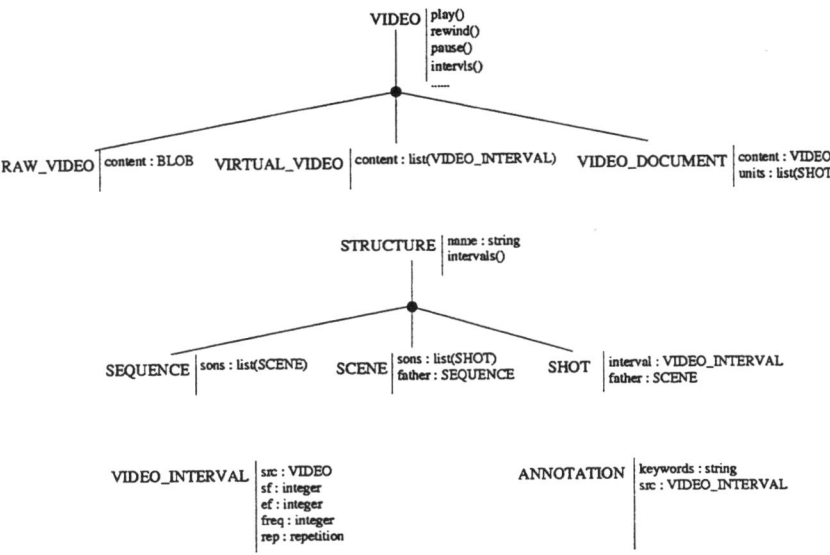

Figure 7. *Video classes hierarchy*

possible to refine the class hierarchy in order to take into account additional formats. Because a raw video is a database object, it can be played using the play method, it can be indexed using our indexing mechanism presented below and finally, it can be queried using the OQL query language.

The second subclass of the VIDEO class is the VIRTUAL_VIDEO subclass. A virtual video is a video constructed from different pieces or segments of video data either raw or virtual. From the end user viewpoint, there is no difference between raw and virtual videos. However, video data belonging to virtual videos are not physically stored in the database. They are generated at presentation time. Virtual videos are defined either graphically or using OQL. As raw videos, a virtual video can be played, indexed and queried. When defining a video interval on a virtual video, we translate it to its corresponding raw video intervals. This operation can be performed immediately after the interval definition (we store raw video interval references) or at presentation time (we store virtual video interval references).

The last subclass of the VIDEO class is the VIDEO_DOCUMENT subclass. It specifies the logical video structure (both for raw and virtual videos). Figure 7 shows the class hierarchy required to capture a customized structure of video data (scene, sequence and shot). The meta-schema captures free structures with more than three levels. We are using a bottom up approach in order to build this structure. The structuring process begins with the shot level, then the scene structure is mapped to the shot level. Finally, the sequence structure is mapped to the scene level. The attributed father in the scene and shot classes allows one to easily traverse the data structure. Actually, the VStorm model is fully implemented on top of the O_2 object-oriented DBMS and has been demonstrated at [LOZ 98a]. As for software functions, we propose a library of classes in order to assist the user in his/her task of creating specific video applications.

5. Conclusion and perspectives

In this paper, we presented a video data model which provides functionalities to store, to manipulate, to query and to present video data. Our video data model considers three dimensions to video data:

– Composition for editing new videos using data already stored in the database.

– Annotation for specifying semantic links between a video segment and a database object or a keyword.

– Structure to provide a way to organize it. We consider that a video is made up of shots which are themselves composed of scenes which can be split into sequences.

We developed an object-oriented DBMS with such capabilities. We developed a library of classes which captures the hierarchical video structure and allows the user to annotate or index video content. This library can be refined in order to create specific indexing structures. The video system supports the edition of new videos from raw video stored in the database without replication.

The video model, its algebraic operators and several associated tools are fully integrated in STORM which is a multimedia presentation system. We have been involved in various applications in areas such as medicine and geographical applications. Actually, we investigate some extensions in order to go beyond present abstract construction.

We plan to use multimedia capabilities in order to manage the layout of video abstracts presentation. We are also interested by querying and delivering videos on the Web and to transform our implementation in a XML type environment.

This paper extends the concept of video abstracting in order to propose different alternatives for saving user time. We argue that a major challenge for digital video systems is their capability of navigating across the semantical view of the video. We propose to use the video structure to dynamically adapt the video content to be compatible with time specification. We also use this structure in order to navigate between scenes and sequences. We used our former work about virtual video in order to implement the dynamic process of video. Most of these works provide a synopsis of a video but without flexibility. Our work is mainly based on trends issues from information retrieval [KUP 95, SAL 94].

REFERENCES

[ADA 96] ADALI S., CANDAN K., CHEN S., EROL K., SUBRAHMANIAN V., "The Advanced Video Information System: Data Structures and Query Processing", *Multimedia Systems*, 1996, p. 172–186.

[AIG 94] AIGRAIN P., JOLY P., "The Automatical Real-time Analysis of Film Editing and Transition Effects and its Applications", *Computer and Graphics*, vol. 18, num. 1, 1994.

[ANS 75] ANSI/X3/SPARC, "Study Group on Database Management Report", *Tsichritzis ed.*, 1975, re-edited in *Information Systems*, Vol. 3, 1978.

[BOR 96] BORECZKY J., ROWE L., "Comparison of Video Shot Boundary Detection Techniques", *Journal of Electronic Imaging*, vol. 5, num. 2, 1996, p. 122–128.

[CAT 93] CATTEL R., Ed., *Object Databases: the ODMG93 Standard*, Morgan-Kaufmann, 1993.

[CHR 94] CHRISTOPHIDES V., ABITEBOUL S., CLUET S., SCHOLL M., "From Structured Documents to Novel Query Facilities", *SIGMOD*, 1994.

[CHR 99] CHRISTEL M. G., OLLIGSCHLAEGER A. M., "Interactive Maps for a Digital Video Library", *Proceedings of the IEEE International Conference on Multimedia Computing and Systems (ICMCS)*, Florence, Italy, June 1999, p. 381–387.

[DEM 98] DEMENTHON D., KOBLA V. D. D., "Video Summarization by Curve Simplification", *Proceedings of the ACM Multimedia Conference*, Bristol, UK, September 1998.

[FLI 95] FLICKNER M., SAWHNEY H., NIBLACK W., ASHLEY J., "Query by Image and Video Content: The QBIC System", *Computer*, 1995.

[GAN 95] GANDHI S., ROBERTSON E., GUCHT D., "Modeling and Querying Primitives for Digital Media", *IEEE International Workshop on Multimedia DBMS*, Minnowbrook Conference Center, Blue Mountain Lake, NY, USA, August 1995.

[HJE 95] HJELSVOLD R., MIDTSTRAUM R., SANDSTA O., "A Temporal Foundation of Video Databases", *International Workshop on Temporal Databases*, Zürich, Switzerland, September 1995.

[HOL 99] HOLLFELDER S., EVERTS A., THIEL U., "Designing for Semantic Access: A Video Browsing System", *Proceedings of the IEEE International Conference on Multimedia Computing and Systems (ICMCS)*, Florence, Italy, June 1999, p. 394–399.

[JIA 98] JIANG H., ELMAGARMID A. K., "Spatial and Temporal Content-based Access to Hypervideo Databases", *The VLDB Journal*, vol. 7, num. 4, 1998, p. 226–238.

[KUP 95] KUPIEC J., PEDERSEN J., CHEN F., "A Trainable Document Summarizer", *18 Annual International ACM SIGIR Conference on Research and Development in Information Retrieval, Text Summarization*, 1995, p. 68–73.

[LAU 94] LAURSEN A., OLKIN J., PORTER M., "Oracle Media Server: Providing Consumer Interactive Access to Multimedia Data", *SIGMOD*, 1994.

[LIE 97] LIENHART R., PFEIFFER S., EFFELSBERG W., "Video Abstracting", *Communications of the ACM*, vol. 40, num. 12, 1997.

[LOZ 98a] Lozano R., Adiba M., Martin H., Mocellin F., "An Object DBMS for Multimedia Presentations including Video Data", *12th European Conference on Object-Oriented Programming (ECOOP '98) Work Shop Reader* (prototype demonstration), Brussels, Belgium, July 1998.

[LOZ 98b] Lozano R., Martin H., "Querying Virtual Videos Using Path and Temporal Expressions", *SAC '98, ACM Symposium on Applied Computing*, Marriott Marquis, Atlanta, Georgia, USA, February 1998.

[LOZ 00] Lozano R., Martin H., "Intégration de Données Vidéo dans un SGBD à Objets", *L'Objet*, vol. 6, num. 3, 2000.

[MAY 97] Maybury M., Merlino A., "Multimedia Summaries of Broadcast News", *International Conference on Intelligent Information Systems*, December 1997.

[MON 81] Monaco J., "How to Read a Film", *The Art, Technology, Language, History and Theory of Film and Media*, 1981, Oxford University Press.

[NAC 99] Nack F., Lindsay A. T., "Everything You Wanted to Know About MPEG-7: Part 1", *IEEE MultiMedia Magazine*, vol. 6, num. 3, 1999, p. 65–77.

[OOM 93] Oomoto E., Tanaka K., "OVID: Design and Implementation of a Video-object Database System", *IEEE Transactions on Knowledge and Data Engineering*, IEEE, August 1993.

[ORG 99] Organisation internationale de normalisation, Coding of mooving pictures and audio (MPEG-7), "DDL Working Draft 1.0", December 1999. http://drogo.cselt.stet.it/mpeg/public/mpeg-7–ddl.zip

[SAA 99] Saarela J., Mérialdo B., "Using Content Models to Build Audio-video Summaries", *Electronic Imaging Conference SPIE'99*, San Jose, USA, January 1999.

[SAC 94] Sack W., Davis M., "IDIC: Assembling Video Sequences from Story Plans and Content Annotations", *IEEE ICMCS*, Boston, MA, 1994.

[SAL 94] Salton G., Allan J., Buckley C., Singhal A., "Automatic Analysis, Theme Generation, and Summarization of Machine-readable Texts", *Science*, vol. 264, 1994, p. 1421–1426.

[VAN 79] Van Rijsbergen C., *Information Retrieval*, Butterworth, London, 1979.

[WEI 95] Weiss R., Duda A., Gifford D., "Composition and Search with a Video Algebra", Spring, Ed., *IEEE multimedia*, p. 12–25, 1995.

[ZHA 93] Zhang H., Kankanhalli A., Smoliar S., "Automatic Partitioning of Full-Motion Video", *Multimedia Systems*, vol. 1, num. 1, 1993, p. 10–28.

Chapter 4

Framework for evaluation of video-to-shots segmentation algorithms: a description scheme for editing work

Rosa Ruiloba and Philippe Joly
Multimedia Team, ASIM-LIP6, Université Pierre et Marie Curie, Paris, France

1. Introduction

Thanks to the evolution of transmission systems, video databases are now more and more accessible for common usage. New applications like push access (information and emission-type filtering) or video online via the Internet, need a quick and precise access to individual documents (information retrieval) in the increasingly advanced video databases. Other applications related to the study and analysis of cinema in cinema schools or document browsing in video archives need a precise indexing process. The results of this process must allow the user to retrieve the information needed, from finding a video document in a database, to finding a given sequence with a given actor. To focus on smaller uniformed segments, and to build up an initial index on a video, a video-to-shot segmentation is performed. This segmentation provides the temporal situation of shots and, in general, several representative frames called *keyframes*. This allows extraction of syntactic information about video documents and to build a synoptic view of the content, like a storyboard. At the same time, the information to be treated can be reduced and limited to keyframes.

In the literature, many different segmentation methods have been proposed. Yet for now, different content sets have been used to evaluate the results. In these conditions the comparison of segmentation methods is impossible. Because of the target application, results are different for different methods and different corpora.

The wide range of video segmentation applications induce various requirements which can be described in terms of types of transition effects to be recognized, accuracy of their detection and localization, and computational time induced. We identify the four following major problems that must be accounted for in the evaluation of video-to-shots segmentation systems:

- Selection and gathering of a corpus (test database).
- Definition of a reference segmentation for this corpus (ground rules).
- Evaluation: comparison of the automated segmentation with a reference segmentation.
- Definition of one or more quality measurement criteria.

The experience of developing such evaluation protocols within the field of speech recognition [DAR 93] suggests that such a development will raise a set of questions on the problem of temporal video segmentation itself. An example of such a validation process is given. In this paper, we first review in detail each of the above issues and discuss their possible solutions. While doing so, we propose a formal context in which temporal video segmentation algorithms can be evaluated.

The video-to-shots segmentation process mostly consists of detecting *transition effects* between *homogeneous segments*. The definition of these entities is rather application dependent. Therefore, there is a strong need (still not satisfied) of a global common evaluation protocol allowing one to test consistently the various algorithms and systems for different targeted applications. In this paper we present different definitions found in the literature and we provide another one to allow easier evaluation and comparison of segmentation results. These definitions will be used to create a Description Scheme for editing work presented in this article.

2. Corpus complexity

In the literature, each segmentation method is tested on a different corpus. Therefore, the comparison between each of them, on the base of the given results, is impossible. To compare segmentation algorithms, it is necessary to provide a same video content set. The selection of a corpus should be independent from the evaluation protocol since it mostly depends on a specific application. However, the protocol must take into account all the corpus characteristics for the evaluation of the difficulty to perform the segmentation, as we will see in Section 5. On the other hand, a corpus can be adapted to evaluate a particular capability of temporal segmentation methods, for example: the detection of a particular type of transition effect, the robustness in relation with objects motion, the ability to work on black and white films or on a particular type of video document.

If our objective is the global evaluation of video-to-shots segmentation, the corpus used must be sufficiently heterogeneous in terms of transition effects type. It must contain some of the common cases of possible errors of segmentation like sequences with fast motion, high illumination changes (explosions, flashes, etc.), different editing rhythms, and so on.

Parameters allowing the evaluation of the corpus complexity should be taken into account to select the elements of the corpus, like, for example: the document size, the heterogeneity in terms of effect types, the number of effects, etc. We propose to use the following parameters as a measure to evaluate the complexity of the corpus:

- Size of the document and number of relevant effects classified by type.
- Document quality: it may affect the segmentation result. Such measures as PSNR, compression rate, or contrast for black and white movies, must be taken into account.
- Histograms of duration of gradual transition effects (like fades and wipes): the results of segmentation algorithms are often affected by the transition duration.
- Editing rhythm: maximum and minimum (and maybe mean and variance) of shot duration.
- Histogram of distances between effects: distance in number of frames between two consecutive effects, and between two consecutive effects of the same type.
- Variation of illumination: this parameter is measured using the maximum and minimum values (or the mean and variance) of differences between histograms of successive frames.
- Motion quantities:
  - Histogram of the Spatial Derivative Difference: a difference exceeding a given threshold may denote the presence of motion or camera work, and a transition effect insertion at this location is likely to be performed.
  - Histogram of the difference between Boundary Phase.
  - Autocorrelation measure.
  - Number of motion pixels on thresholded difference between images: the difference between two images points out the changes in the images. We considered only changes above a fixed threshold.

Variation of illumination and motion quantities are not global parameters but are locally computed. Even so, they are important parameters to take into account when evaluating the segmentations quality. It may explain why errors are made at certain points and then permit the weighting of such errors (see Section 5). If the difference between the frames located before and after an effect is above a certain threshold, the detection of the transition is easy and an error can be seriously considered. On the other hand, if this difference is important between two frames within a shot (e.g. flash), a transition effect insertion is likely to be made at this place. In Table 1, we present the values of the above parameters for corpora of different degrees of complexity.

2.1. Video content sets

There are not many video content sets for evaluation purposes, in contrast with the great quantity of video documents available now on the Internet. Different consortia have elaborate specific corpora, like MPEG-7 content set [MPE 99]. But the access to such a corpus is generally restricted due to copyright aspects of usage. Some of the results presented in [RUI 99b] summarized in this article were

Table 1. A difficult corpus (resp. easy) will have a great number of gradual transitions (resp. a small number). The duration of these transitions will be very short (ex. 4 frames) or very large (resp. a medium duration). The shot duration will have the same characteristics (too short or too large). Consequently, the effects will be very distant (90 frames) or very close (10 frames).

CorpusType	#Eff.C	#Eff.Gr.	Hist. grad. tran.	Edit R.	Hist. dist.
Easy Corpus	95 cuts	5 diss.	0-5-0	M:250 m:25 Fr.	0-10-90
Difficult Corpus	5cuts	95 diss.	47-0-48	M:500 m:8 Fr.	90-0-10

obtained using the WG-10 corpus developed within the French inter-laboratory research group ISIS. This corpus contains 8 videos of a total duration of 172 minutes. It includes several TV news, various advertising, and TV series. The results of the works made on this corpus are accessible on the website [GTI 99].

3. Definition of a reference segmentation

To evaluate the response of a system, we must compare the results with the ground rules. It is this ground rule that we call reference segmentation. This reference is sometimes given by the script or the Edit Decision List (EDL) of the video document when it is available but, frequently, it must be built manually. The EDL is rarely available and the format is mostly private and only understood by particular editing softwares. In order to reduce the human error and subjectivity in the manual segmentation, several evaluators must work concurrently on the same task. The results must be cross-checked to produce a reliable reference. Different "evaluators" may have different definitions of transitions, and some mistakes may be introduced. Moreover, for a given person, the criteria used for the segmentation can change during a long segmentation process. In order to obtain consistent results, the *definition of a transition effect* must be given in the clearest and most unambiguous terms.

3.1. Cross-checking results

We choose to start to build the reference by checking an initial automatic segmentation result. A human "evaluator" checks whether the gathered keyframes (the last frame of a shot and the first frame of the next shot, for example) effectively delimit a transition effect or belong to the same shot. The complete video sequence is then used to check the presence of detected effects and to mark any possible missed transition effects. The results may be influenced by the evaluated method and the application domain, and may consider only a few types of effects. In this case, this result may be unreliable to validate other segmentation techniques. A reference segmentation must be independent of algorithms and applications. In our experimental work two teams participate with us in building the reference:

CLIPS-IMAG[1] and the INA[2]. Each team was working on a different automatic segmentation method. The results of these methods were evaluated over the same corpus [GTI 99]. The building reference process consisted in checking the difference between the three manual evaluations. Where a difference appeared, the local transition was checked against its strict definition and then was kept or discarded.

After the validation of our automatic segmentation results, about 16.22% of the transitions were checked due to differences between validation results produced by each team.

3.2. Definition of segmentation items

For a given corpus, the results of several algorithms may be different due to the different definitions of transition effects on which the segmentations are based, and due to the fact that the algorithmic approaches are different.

3.2.1. The problem of a clear definition of transition effects

To describe the video content from the point of view of the editing work, we need a clear definition of transition effects and a correct description of each type of transition. These definitions allow us to build a reliable segmentation reference. Different existing definitions for automatic shot segmentations are, in general, application dependent. We decided to use definitions used in the technical field of audiovisual production. In our first collaborative work, three types of transition effects were defined: *cuts, dissolves* and *others*. This experience showed that giving a formal definition is not always straightforward, even for such obvious cases. For instance, problems appeared when classifying "temporal discontinuities" happening in "visual jingles", stroboscopic effects, logo appearance, etc. Are they cuts? Other transition effects? In the experimentation they were labelled as cuts but another label called "semantic level" was added. This label was used to highlight the importance of a transition effect ("1" for cuts between meaningful shots and "0" for cuts in a stroboscopic effect, for example). In this context, a transition was counted only if it corresponded to a transition applied to the complete frame.

In Section 9 of this article, we provide more precise definitions which allow us to correctly describe video editing work.

3.2.2. Definition of a common description format

In the preliminary experimental work, different file formats were used by the authors to store the results of automatic segmentations and the reference. We used a straightforward text format in a first approach. Then, formats more suited to the description such as rdf were used. Finally, XML has been chosen to describe the

---

1. 385, rue de la Bibliothèque, BP53, 38041 Grenoble Cedex 9, France
2. Institut National de l'Audiovisuel (French National Institute of Audiovisual Archives). 4, avenue de l'Europe, 94366 Bry-sur-Marne, France

video document. Its proximity to the future MPEG-7 DDL was one of the main reasons for this choice. We used this language to produce a description scheme (DS) of transition effects on the base of their definitions. This DS is presented later in this article (see Section 8).

3.2.3. Comparison with the reference segmentation

The comparison provides three types of errors:

– **Detection error:** this shows the transitions in the reference (all types mixed up) which are not detected and the detected transitions which do not appear in the reference.

– **Classification error:** this takes into account the type of correctly detected transitions (the overlap between the reference and the automatic segmented transitions is large enough). An error is detected if the type of transition is not the same between the automatic segmentation and the reference.

– **Location error:** this measures the difference in relation to localization of gradual transition. The error is computed over transitions that are correctly detected.

On the other hand, the comparison between the reference (which is supposed to contain only correct information) and the result can provide different results regarding definitions of correctness and error. We must define the error and correctness in the specific context of the applications considered. For example, a reference segmentation may describe cuts, fades, dissolves and wipes and the segmentation algorithm may only be able to detect cuts and fades without any distinction between fades and cross-dissolves. We must decide if the classification of wipes as fades are errors or not.

Additional rules must be defined in order to determine whether an effect is correctly matched to the reference. For cuts, the error computation is straightforward, but it is not the case for gradual transitions, particularly for fades and dissolves where the limits cannot be clearly fixed during a manual segmentation.

In the literature, different choices have been made. For example [LUP 98] considers a minimum overlap of one frame and measures the recall and precision of gradual transitions, see Section 4.1.3. In [HAM 95], an overlap measure is computed to match the segments (T_1 and T_2) corresponding to the shots of the reference and of the automatic segmentation, respectively:

$$O(T_1, T_2) = |t_{1b} - t_{2e}| - (|t_{1b} - t_{2b}| + |t_{1e} - t_{2e}|),$$ [1]

where $T_1 = [t_{1b}, t_{1e}]$ and $T_2 = [t_{2b}, t_{2e}]$. In our preliminary experimental work, it has been decided that a dissolve effect was correctly detected if and only if it partly overlaps by at least 50% with the correct one.

In our experimentation, it has to be decided if a confusion between a *dissolve* and an *other effect* or between a *cut* and a *very short dissolve* should be counted as an error or not. Such rules, parameterizable in order to take into account the application field details, were implemented in software by Georges Quénot of CLIPS-IMAG, which is able to automatically count the number of insertions and deletions for each type of effect ([GTI 99]).

4. Selection of quality measure criteria

The correct detections and errors are combined in different manners to produce quality measures allowing comparison of different methods. Below, some examples of the formulas that have already been proposed to evaluate temporal segmentation methods are presented. Some problems and advantages of these formulas are also discussed.

4.1. State of the art

4.1.1. Accuracy

A simple expression to compute the accuracy is proposed by Aigrain and Joly in [AIG 94]. It is equivalent to a measure commonly used for the evaluation of speech recognition systems [DAR 93]:

$$\text{Accuracy} = \frac{N_T - (N_D + N_I)}{N_T} = \frac{N_C - N_I}{N_T}, \qquad [2]$$

where N_T, N_D, N_I and N_C are respectively the number of transition effects present in the reference segmentation, the number of transition effects deleted, inserted and correctly found by the tested system.

Counter-intuitive results may be obtained using this measure (Accuracy $\# 0$) when $N_I > N_C$ or $(N_D + N_I) > N_T$. This may happen when the number of errors is greater or equal to the number of transitions. Moreover, it is important to include the size of the video sequence in the evaluation of a segmentation method because the number of errors may potentially be equal to the number of frames N_F. The previous measure does not take into account either the complexity of the video sequence or its size.

4.1.2. Error rate

Corridoni and Del Bimbo [COR 95] propose a measure that evaluates the error rate (insertion and deletion of transition effects) over all the results of the segmentation algorithm:

$$\text{Error Rate} = \frac{N_D + N_I}{N_T + N_I} = \frac{N_D + N_I}{N_C + N_D + N_I}. \qquad [3]$$

Here again, this measure does not include the complexity and size of the test video sequence. This measure is not adequate for the evaluation and the comparison of various methods because it implicitly gives more importance to deleted transition effects than to inserted ones. This importance is not weighted with an explicit factor and is therefore difficult to assess. For example, for a video sequence containing 10 transition effects, we obtain an error rate = 1/3 if the segmentation technique produces 5 effect insertions (i.e. $N_T = 10, N_D = 0, N_I = 5$). By contrast, the error rate increases (error rate = ½) in the case of 5 deletions (i.e. $N_T = 10, N_D = 5, N_I = 0$).

4.1.3. Recall and Precision

The measure used by Boreczky and Rowe [BOR 96] can be applied in different contexts, particularly in the context of information retrieval. They propose the Recall (which is the ratio between desired and found items), and the Precision (which is the ratio of found items that are expected).

$$\text{Recall} = \frac{N_C}{N_C + N_D} \quad \text{Precision} = \frac{N_C}{N_C + N_I}. \quad [4]$$

These two previous parameters are strongly correlated and are not normalized, so they do not provide any interesting clues for the comparison. An algorithm that makes many errors receives worse precision and recall scores than an algorithm that detects an effect for each frame. In general, graphs of Recall values are displayed as a function of Precision for different threshold values. Different Recall values are given for a given Precision value since these measures are, in general, compensated: if the evaluated segmentation method is very strict, the number of deleted transition effects increases while the number of inserted effects decreases. The consequence is a decreasing Recall value against an increasing Precision value.

A modification of these parameters is proposed in [LUP 98] to measure the detection of gradual transitions involving several frames: the recall and precision cover. The recall represents the ratio between the overlap (in frames) of the detected effect and the real one, over the real effect duration. The precision is the ratio between the overlap and the detected transition duration:

$$Recall_{cover} = \frac{b}{a} \quad Precision_{cover} = \frac{b}{c}, \quad [5]$$

where a is the duration of the real transition, c the detected one and b the overlap between both effects.

4.1.4. Time boundary and classification errors

Hampapur and Jain consider two of the error types presented in Section 3.2.3: detection error and classification error. They proposed a very interesting application-oriented measure [HAM 95]. It allows one to increase the weight corresponding to a given error type according to the application.

$$E(V,V') = E_{SB} * W_{SB} + E_{SC} * W_{SC},$$ [6]

where V: $\{S_1, S_2 ... S_N\}$ is the manual video segmentation in N segments (S_n), $V' = \{S'_1, S'_2 ... S'_K\}$ is the automated video segmentation, E_{SB} is the error in terms of temporal segment limit defined by the transition effects, W_{SB} is the weight of the temporal limit error relating to the application, E_{SC} is the error of mis-classification of transition effects and W_{SC} is the weight of the classification error. The segment limit and classification errors are computed:

$$E_{SB}(V,V') = \frac{\sum_{i=1}^{n} e_i(S_i, S'_i)}{Length(V)} + \frac{n' + k'}{\lambda},$$

$$e_i(T_1, T_2) = |t_{1b} - t_{2b}| + |t_{1e} - t_{2e}|.$$

$$E_{SC}(V,V') = \frac{\sum_{i=1}^{n} e_{sc}(S_i, S'_i)}{n} + \frac{n' + k'}{\lambda},$$ [7]

where n is the number of segments, $\lambda = n$ for under and equal segmentation and $\lambda = Length(V)$ for over segmentation, n' and k' are the number of unassigned segments in V and V' after the comparison between reference and automatic segmentation, l_{S2} and l_{S2} are the classification labels of the segments and $e_{sc} = 1$ if l_{S1} are different to l_{S2}. This performance measure is related to the application domain and is able to compute the errors made by most of the segmentation methods. However, the boundary segment error is very difficult to evaluate in the case of *dissolve* effects. The manual segmentation is therefore not reliable in this case. The transitions inserted and deleted ($n' + k'$) are considered in the boundary error but also in the classification error. We consider that the classification error is only computed over the correctly detected transitions. On the other hand, the importance of insertions and deletions ($n' + k'$)/λ change depending on the fact that the document is under or over segmented (because λ change). Eickeler and Rigoll in [EIC 00] propose a solution to this problem and compare the result with a proposed error measure.

4.2. Proposed measures

Every application will give more or less importance to one or several of the three different types of errors: detection, classification and location. We propose here some measures to overcome the shortcomings of the preceding ones.

4.2.1. Classification error probability

The error classification is computed only over well detected transitions. The classification error is related to the type of detected transition. Again, this measure is not meaningful for all systems, but only for segmentation and classification methods. Most of the methods only differentiate a little set of transitions: mainly cuts or cuts and dissolves. We propose to weight every kind of error. We consider four types of transitions: cuts, dissolves (including fade-in and fade-out), wipes and a last group called "other". Of course, a more detailed classification can be made.

$$P_{ClassificationError} \quad = W_{CEr} * P(detectingCUT|Dissolve|Wipe|Other)$$
$$+W_{DEr} * P(detectingDISSOLVE|Cut|Wipe|Other)$$
$$+W_{wEr} * P(detectingWIPE|Cut|Dissolve|Other)$$
$$+W_{OEr} * P(detectingOTHER|Cut|Dissolve|Wipe). \ [8]$$

4.2.2. Insertion probability

The insertion probability is the probability that a transition effect is detected where no effect is present:

$$P(\text{insertion}) = P(\text{detection|no effect}) = \frac{N_I}{N_F - N_T}. \qquad [9]$$

4.2.3. Deletion probability

It is the probability of failing in detecting an effect when the effect exists:

$$P(\text{deletion}) = P(\text{no detection|effect}) = \frac{N_D}{N_T}. \qquad [10]$$

Similar equations can be found in [HAU 98] to evaluate the stories segmentation in news videos. It is based on an original formula from [BEE 97] used to evaluate the text segmentation. What we call insertions and deletions are respectively called "false alarm" and "miss" in that article:

$$P_{Miss} = \frac{\sum_{i=1}^{N-k} \delta_{hyp}(i, i+k)(1 - \delta_{ref}(i, i+k))}{\sum_{i=1}^{N-k}(1 - \delta_{ref}(i, i+k))}, \qquad [11]$$

$$P_{FalseAlarm} = \frac{\sum_{i=1}^{N-k}(1 - \delta_{hyp}(i, i+k))\delta_{ref}(i, i+k)}{\sum_{i=1}^{N-k}(\delta_{ref}(i, i+k))}, \qquad [12]$$

where $\delta(i, j) = 1$ if i and j are from the same story and is equal to zero otherwise. The segmentation of the news links every word to a story. The formula compares the results for the automatic(hyp) and reference(ref) segmentations.

In the case of video-to-shots segmentation, the words are the frames and the stories are the shots. It should be noted that equations [10] and [9] are basically equivalent to equations [11] and [12].

4.2.4. Error probability

We propose two measures to compute the global error. First, the classical error definition used in detection theory in the signal processing domain and a second measure that allows us to weight both insertion and deletion errors.

4.2.5. Classical error probability

In detection theory, the error probability is the probability to produce a false alarm or not to detect a symbol. That is:

$$P_e = P_{Miss} + P_{FalseAlarm} = P(\text{no detection}|\text{effect}) + P(\text{detection}|\text{no effect})$$

$$= \frac{N_D}{N_T} + \frac{N_I}{N_F - N_T}. \qquad [13]$$

4.2.6. Adaptive error probability

There are a lot of applications using video-to-shots segmentation. Each one needs different quality levels. For example in some cases missing a gradual transition may be less convenient than adding a false transition.

The importance of each kind of error can be modified by changing their weights: W_{FA} (for the false alarm) and W_M (for the missed transitions) in the following formula:

$$P_e = W_M * P_{Miss} + W_{FA} * P_{FalseAlarm}, \qquad [14]$$

where W_M and W_{FA} take values between 0.0 and 1.0 and $W_M + W_{FA} = 1$. A new error probability can be computed from the previous formula: the probability to make an error (deletion or insertion) when an error is possible. For this probability the weights take the next values: $W_M = P(effect)$ and $W_{FA} = P(noeffect)$. We consider that the temporal segmentation methods can make a detection error on each video frame.

This expression would give, in general, more importance to insertion errors than deletions because the number of transitions is lower than the number of intra-shot frame.

$$P(e|ep) = \begin{aligned} &P(effect) * P(nodetection|effect) + \\ &P(noeffect) * P(detection|noeffect) = \frac{N_D + N_I}{N_F}. \end{aligned} \qquad [15]$$

4.2.7. Correctness probability

This is the probability to detect a transition effect when it exists and not to detect it when it does not exist. We can give more importance to each of these situations by using weights ($k1$, $k2$). It is the complementary probability of the previous one.

$P(\text{correction})=$ $k1 * P(\text{detection}|\text{effect}) + k2 * P(\text{no detection}|\text{no effect}) =$

$k1 * (1 - P(\text{deletion})) + k2 * (1 - P(\text{insertion})) =$ [16]

$(k1 + k2)(1 - (k1' * P(\text{deletion}) + k2' * P(\text{insertion}))),$

Where $k1$, $k2$, $k1'$ and $k2'$ take values between 0.0 and 1.0 and $k1 + k2 = 1$. For the results shown in Table 1, we used $k1 = k2 = k1' = k2' = 0.5$.

All these proposed measures take into account both the total number of transition effects (N_T) and the total number of frames in the given sequence (N_F). This makes these measures more robust to the problems encountered before while using the previous definitions.

4.2.8. Location error

The location error computes the distance between the position of a gradual transition to the reference and the position of the matched transition in the resulting segmentation. Two measures are proposed:

4.2.9. Duration error

This is the normalized difference between the duration in number of frames or time units:

$$Error_{Duration} = \frac{|S_{ref} - S_{seg}|}{S_{ref}},$$ [17]

where S_{ref} and S_{seg} are, respectively, the duration (in number of frames or time units) of the gradual transition in the reference segmentation and in the automatic one.

4.2.10. Center location error

$$Error_{Location} = \frac{|C_{ref} - C_{seg}|}{S_{ref}},$$ [18]

where C_{ref} and C_{seg} are, respectively, middle point (in number of frames or time units) of the gradual transition in the reference segmentation and in the automatic one. The error is normalized in relation to the size of the gradual transition. A shifting for a long transition is less important than for a shorter one.

5. Complexity of the detection of a transition effect

The complexity of the detection must be included within the evaluation process in order to weight the possible types of errors made. The cases of segmentation errors are different for different segmentation algorithms. High illumination changes and fast motion may produce insertions in many algorithms. However, in general, an error is more important if the transition is clear: between very different frames, different characters, or different places.

We propose several measures to evaluate the algorithms in relation to the different difficult cases:

– Insertion, deletion and correction probabilities related to changes in image content. This results in defining the probability of the insertion of a transition effect over the histogram difference and the probability of correct detection over the histogram difference, respectively given as:

$$P(\text{insertion} \mid \Delta H) P(\text{deletion} \mid \Delta H) \text{ and } P(\text{correct detection} \mid \Delta H).$$

– Insertion, deletion and correction probabilities related to motion quantity. The measure proposed in Section 2, can be used as an indicator for "motion quantity".

– Insertion, deletion and correction probabilities related to the rhythm. The rhythm can be given by the histogram of shots durations.

6. Method complexity evaluation: computing time

In order to compare the temporal segmentation methods, it is important to use a measure of complexity in relation to the induced computing time, the need of learning and the adaptation of the threshold with the considered document. Computing time is the time spent to obtain the segmentation of a document. This time is dependent of the computer architectures. Available common architecture must be given as reference. If learning is needed and made off line and once for all types of sequences, it is not penalizing.

7. Evaluation results of some temporal video segmentation methods

We have evaluated some classical segmentation methods and methods developed by the members of Working Group 10 of the ISIS Coordinate Research Program mentioned in Section 3.

In Table 2 we present the results obtained for the classical methods. The methods are: histogram difference, intensities difference, difference between the addition of intensities, χ^2 formula, χ^2 formula over the blocks (see previous measures in [NAG 92]), histogram intersection of [WOL 95], invariant moments difference of [DAI 95], thresholded intensities variation of [ZHA 93] and correlation rate proposed in [UED 91]. For every quality measure, it shows the mean values obtained over eight documents. Since not all the tested methods are able to handle every possible type of effects, only cuts were used in our evaluation. All values are presented as percentages. Looking at this table, we can see that

Table 2. *Several reliability measures of cut segmentation*

Method	Accur.	Prec.	Recall	Error R.	Ins. Pr	Del. Pr	Error Pr	Corr. Pr
Hist. Diff.	−157.2	24.88	78.0	76.75	2.11	22.03	2.29	87.92
Int. Diff.	37.0	65.48	78.1	44.67	0.37	21.90	0.56	88.86
Som. Int.	77.8	90.85	86.5	20.39	0.07	13.45	0.19	93.23
χ^2 Form.	−27.9	41.67	69.9	64.66	0.87	30.09	1.14	84.51
χ^2 Block	−38.5	40.88	86.5	61.55	1.12	13.45	1.23	92.70
Hist. Inter.	−373.3	16.44	91.5	83.80	4.18	8.49	4.22	93.66
Invar. Diff.	1.2	50.29	95.3	50.90	0.84	4.66	0.88	97.24
Thres. Int.	−137.2	21.92	53.6	81.56	1.71	46.38	2.11	75.94
Corr. Rate	−1462.5	3.50	55.2	96.59	13.65	44.81	13.93	70.76

some measures used in the literature are difficult to interpret. Among others, accuracy presents negative values.

8. Description scheme for video editing work

We propose a description scheme to describe an audiovisual document from a video editing point of view. It is based on techniques used in the video edition domain. The main objective of this DS is to give a complete, modular and extensible description of the structure of the video documents. One of the interests of this approach is the hierarchical organization, with different levels of granularity. The goals are:

– Evaluation of video-to-shots segmentation algorithms.
– Video document indexing and analysis.
– Standard description of the Edit Decision Lists (EDL)[GAR 88].
– Elaboration of editing patterns (currently available editing tools do not provide any model or editing style).

This DS tries to facilitate the building of a reference segmentation and consequently the evaluation of algorithms. It is intended to be generic in the sense that it supports a large number of applications which need a description of the editing. Moreover, to be able to evaluate further works which will detect more sophisticated editing effects such as "splitscreens" or localized effects, the proposed DS must be as complete as possible regarding the editing work. That leads obviously to an ability to handle functionalities for digital editing boards. Very detailed elements of the proposed DS are provided to define editing patterns that allow several possible reconstructions of films. It can provide different editing models for the same document depending on, for example, the target audience.

Standards as SMPTE [SMP 93] allow one to describe EDLs but no standard exists for the analytic description of editing work. This work shows how MPEG-7 could be used to compensate this lack of formal language [JOL 99], [RUI 99a] and

[RUI 00]. Other solutions and languages are used to describe video content and content queries as in [ARD 99]. Following [MAR 99], a description scheme (DS) specifies the structure and semantics of the relationships between its components, which may be both descriptors (D) and DSs. A description follows the DS (structure) and contains a set of descriptor values (instantiations) that describe the data. The DS, D and description are created using Description Scheme Definition Language (DDL). We used MPEG-7 DDL version 1.1 in this paper. (Figure 1 refers.)

In this second part, we will only introduce the main concepts and properties of the proposed DS in order to justify its usefulness. Due to the syntax size, we will not present the full specification.

9. Definitions

Video document analysis requires a definition of *shots* and *transition effects* as accurate and complete as possible. This definition is an ambitious task regarding the evolution of editing softwares. An enormous quantity of effects is now possible and a classification of these effects is not always clearly identified.

In [GOL 92], we find the following definition for a shot: "Film portion recorded by the camera between the beginning and the end of a recording. In a final movie, the pastes limit a shot".

Hampapur in [HAM 94] provide another definition of a shot: "An image sequence which presents continuous action which appears to be from a single operation of the camera [DAV 91]".

The facilities brought by virtual edition make this definition too ambiguous and sometimes false. An editing process consists of connecting and mixing different recordings at different times. We can mix, for example, frames recorded at the same time by different cameras. Recordings will be connected by *transition effects* and mixed by *composition effects*. Then, a shot will be formed by one video recording (or several if there is a composition rush) between two transition effects. These recordings are called *rushes* in the film industry. An example is the well-known composition rush called "splitscreen". The screen is split into several parts, each one displaying different rushes.

A rush can be a sequence of frames showing only text or a still picture, used in composition rushes.

We have modified the initial shot definitions to take into account *composition rushes*, *composition effects* and *internal transition effects*. The main characteristic that allows one to make the difference between a *global transition effect* (between shots) and an *internal transition effect* (between rushes) is the frame area that is affected by the effect. Here is a definition of a *global transition effect* and consequently of a shot.

– Definition of a global transition effect
A global transition effect is a visual effect that covers the whole frame. This effect

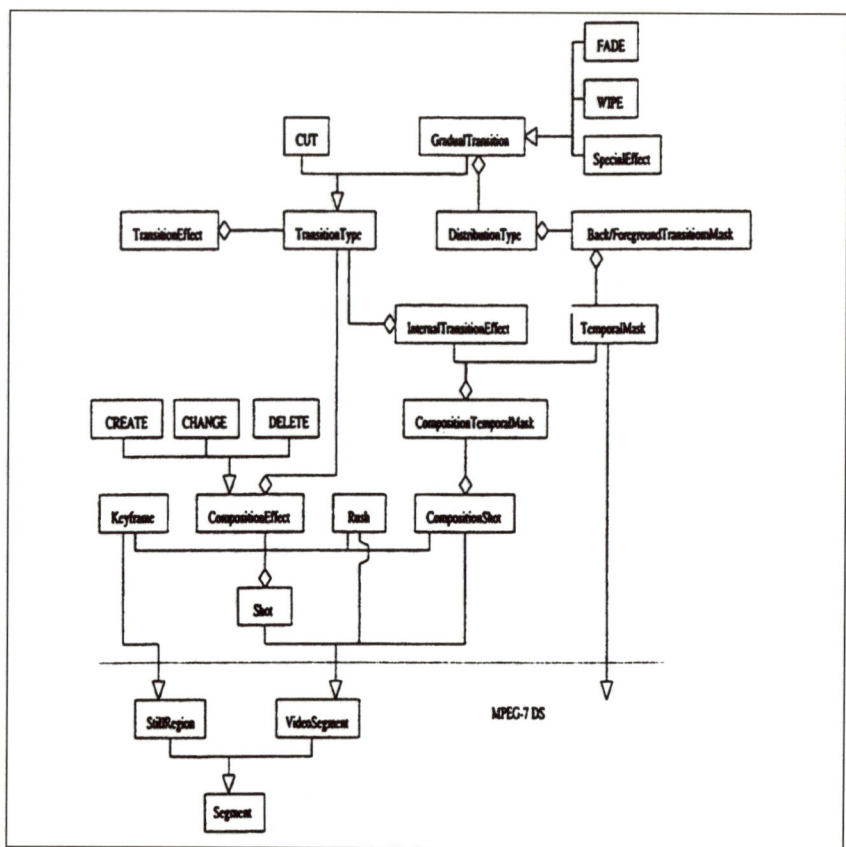

Figure 1. *This is a UML graphic of some of the elements of this DS. The DSs and Ds are represented by rectangles. The triangles points out the DS or D inherited by the DS or D at the opposite side of the drawn link. The lines starting with a diamond link a DS to one of its components.*

supposes the rush (or all the rushes) on the screen disappears before the effect, and that new ones, which where not visible until that moment, appear after the effect. The given definition is proposed to remain as close as possible to the actual process of film editing.

– Definition of a shot

A shot is a sequence of frames that forms a temporal unit in the final video document. It can be seen as the edited version of a rush (or rushes). The temporal boundaries are defined by the presence of global transition effects. One or several rushes may compose a shot involving composition and internal transition effects.

– Definition of a frame

The smallest temporal unit of a video document associated with a visual semantic. Each image in the video stream is a frame.

– Definition of a rush

A frame sequence before being possibly assembled with other rushes to build a shot (or another intermediate rush).

– Definition of a composition rush

A composition rush is a particular case of a rush that combines several rushes in the same frame (for an example, see Figure 4). We can find several compositions in the same shot which are linked by *composition effects*.

– Definition of composition effect

There are three types of composition effects: a composition effect that introduces a composition rush (in that case the rush on the full frame before the effect becomes a part of the composition rush); a composition effect that ends a composition rush (the rush on the full frame at the end of the effect was a part of the composition rush); the last type is a transition between two composition rushes.

One example of the first type is the introduction of a text with the anchor's name in broadcasted TV news. This text can be introduced gradually by a dissolve effect which is considered as a composition effect.

The rushes that take part in a composition rush appear in the frames by a transition effect similar to the one which links up the shots. But, as far as their characteristics may slightly differ from those of the global transition effects, they are introduced in that description scheme as a separate class of objects called composition effects.

The regions taking part in a composition rush may move within the frame. This motion is not considered as a composition effect introducing a new composition rush. We only consider a composition effect when a subregion of the whole frame appears or disappears.

– Definition of an internal transition effect

This effect has got all the characteristics of a global transition effect excepted that it happens only in a subregion (see Figure 2). Also both differ by the type of the

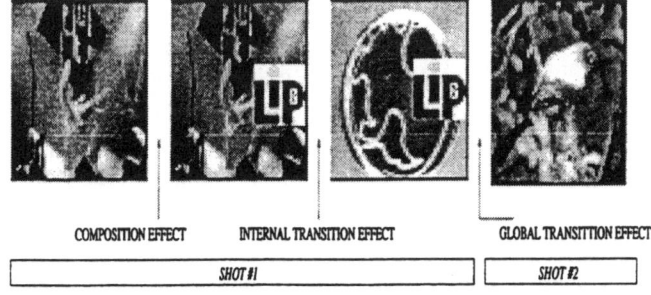

COMPOSITION EFFECT   INTERNAL TRANSITION EFFECT   GLOBAL TRANSITION EFFECT

SHOT #1   SHOT #2

Figure 2. The first shot contains two different effects. First, there is a competition effect of type cut: an incrustation appears in a subpart of the frame. The second is an internal transition effect: the incrustation is not affected by the effect. A global transition effect of type cut introduces the second shot.

involved video segments (only rushes for the internal one and shots for the second one).

9.1. The DS refinements

For editing purposes only, the evaluation features in the DS are not required. For that reason, we present the *VideoToShotsSegmentation DS* as a specialization of the *Editing Work DS* which introduces the elements used to compare segmentation methods. The following DSs are based on the previous definitions.

10. Editing work DS

This DS is composed of two fundamental groups: the shot group and the transition effect group. Analytic and semantic descriptions in relation to the shot subject, picture content, etc, are possible using *Annotation* or other higher level DSs proposed in MPEG-7 framework. This DS allows one to describe the editing work made by an editing software, using more detailed descriptors of *Shot* and *TransitionEffect* DSs. In the DS, the higher (resp. the lower) is the element of description, the more analytic (resp. synthetic) is the information. Parameters of the editing effects are low-level descriptors; parameters of the global structure of a document are high-level descriptors in the same DS.

There are different ways to combine the rushes, in relation to the style of the film or the type of the focused audience, for example. This DS contains an *EditorInformation DS* which provides information about the objectives of a particular editing work. It gives the editor's name(s), the date of the editing work, its classification among the editing work types, the edition purposes (target audience) and the required material. This DS contains also the next descriptors:

– **Id**: an identifier that allows one to differentiate one description among others (id condition in XML).

– **MediaProfile DS**: it describes a specific format resolution and media. It contains information in relation to the video document. This is an MPEG-7 DS.

10.1. VideoToShotsSegmentation DS: evaluation and validation

We differentiate between two processes to measure the errors of a segmentation algorithm: the validation and the evaluation process. The validation needs to review the video segment corresponding to shots and transitions detected to judge whether the segmentation is correct or not. Successive validations allow us to produce a reference segmentation. The evaluation achieves the comparison of the results of the automatic segmentation with the reference segmentation. For detection errors, we determine whether the transition is correct, inserted or deleted.

VideoToShotsSegmentation DS is a specification of the Editing Work DS. Specific DSs are added to achieve validation and evaluation tasks: VideotoShotsAutomaticSegmentationInfo, VideotoShots ValidationSegmentation and VideotoShotsEvaluationSegmentation. A sequence of TransitionEffect DSs is provided and a sequence of DSs of shots is also specified, but its presence is not required for evaluation tasks. During the evaluation process, only the localization and type of the global transition effects are taken into account.

The VideoToShotsSegmentation DS is added to handle the validation and evaluation information produced during the evaluation process. A part of this information is added to the TransitionEffect and Shot DSs (VideotoShotsAutomatic SegmentationInfo, VideotoShotsValidationSegmentation and VideotoShot-Evaluation Segmentation).

VideotoShotsAutomaticSegmentationInfo DS provides information about the date, the software and the author of the automatic segmentation described.

VideotoShots ValidationSegmentation DS gives the date and the author of the validation process. It also provides a sequence of added global transition effects (SetOfAddedTransitions) with, eventually, a reference to the shot which was undersegmented by the automatic segmentation.

VideotoShotsEvaluationSegmentation DS provides information about the evaluation process. It contains previous DSs and adds a reference to the reference segmentation used in the evaluation process.

10.2. TransitionEffect DS

The TransitionType DS represents the type of transition, different types of transition, localization of the transition and its type. The localization is given in two ways: with a time value or with the identification of the previous and the next shots. The first expression is more useful for the evaluation process, where the localization of the transitions in the automatic segmentation must be compared with the reference one. The TransitionType DS represents the type of transition. Different types of transition like cuts or fades will inherit this DS and give the transition effect description. This DS contains an "ID" and the following information:

   – **TransitionEffectEvaluation D**: this indicates if the transition was correctly detected or inserted or deleted by the segmentation algorithm. It contains a SegmentError D which allows us to measure the location transition error. This parameter is only optional and used to build the reference or to evaluate a segmentation.

   – **StartTime DS**: this gives the beginning of the transition and eventually its duration.

   – **TransEffectShotRelationShipNode DS**: this indicates which are the previous and the next shots in a global transition effect.

   – **TransitionType DS**: this is the type of a transition effect. It is an abstract DS (as an abstract class in an object-oriented language) which only contains the transition name. Particular transition types will inherit TransitionType DS and will add some needed parameters.

The Transition Type DS describes how the rushes are combined: as a cut, as a fade, and so on. Every level transition mentioned previously (composition effect, global transition effects and internal transition effects) can be created using these "transition types". They will contain a Transition Type DS.

The TransitionEffectEvaluation D provides the delay between the actual and the detected start of the transition (delayStart) and the difference of duration (diffDuration) in relation with the reference segmentation. Information about the classification error are given by TransitionTypeSegmentationError, which inherits SegmentationError. It provides the correct type of transition (validType) and the origin of the error (ShotSegmentationErrorCause). ShotSegmentationErrorCause D takes the following values: slowMotion, fastMotion, InternalTransitionEffect, VideoCompositionTransitionEffect, flashes, illuminationChanges and darkscene.

10.3. VideoCompositionEffect DS

This DS describes composition effects as defined in Section 9. Because of the similarity with global transition effects, it contains an id, the StartTime, and the TransitionType DS, like the TransitionEffect DS. Another attribute gives the type of the composition effect.

This is an abstract DS and it cannot be instantiated. We define three types of VideoCompositionEffect DSs which can be instantiated. These three kinds of composition effects are proposed to address the three possible combinations of rushes and composition rushes (see Section 9).

10.4. InternalTransitionEffect DS

This DS describes internal transition effects, according to the already given definitions. Its content is similar to the TransitionEffect DS, except that it refers to the next and previous rushes and not to shots (InterTransRushRelationshipNode). An illustration of this effect is shown in Figure 2.

10.5. GradualTransition DS and masking

We can identify two types of transitions: abrupt and gradual ones. The first type corresponds to cuts. Fades or wipes are considered as gradual transitions. We call gradual transitions, transitions that affect progressively different parts of the begining or of the ending frames of a video segment. This DS is provided to describe different gradual transition types which add specific parameters to the ones present in this DS. The description is based on editing cinema techniques, where different masks (which were actually pieces of glass) are used to produce some optical effects. A fade to black is obtained by using a set of specific masks, with different gradual levels of transparency.

We define in the same way "digital masks" (or mattes) to be applied to the shot frames to build the transitions. These masks are called TransitionTemporalMasks.

Two types of masks are possible. The first possibility is a video document where each pixel intensity gives the transparency to be applied to the frames during the transition. The second possibility is a 2-D or 3-D shape bearing a rigid or non-rigid motion. For example, it can be used to map a rush on a sphere in a subpart of the screen. This mask, defined as a shape and a motion (with descriptors like those proposed by languages like BIFS or VRML) needs a transparency matrix. It also needs a Limit D, which describes if the limit is fuzzy, its color and its size. For both types of mask description, we must point out if the contained frames are **masked**: the mask is applied over the frame; **mapped**: the frame is adapted to the mask dimensions; or **tracked**: the frame is stick over the visible mask and it moves with it.

An example of "tracked" frames is the particular wipe called "push". In Figure 3, the three cases are shown. The description of gradual transitions inherits Transition-Type DS plus the next descriptors:

- **TransitionDuration DS**: this is the duration of a transition effect.
- **BeginningFrames and EndingFrames DS**: is the number of frames starting and ending the transition effect. They are the number of frames of previous and next shots used to build the transition.
- **IntensityEffectParameters DS**: represents the function used to modify the intensity of the pixels in a frame. This modification is made during the editing process to make the connected frames of the sequences (shots or rushes) more similar. This step is called calibration.
- **DistributionType DS**: describes the way in which the previous and the next video segments are combined to produce the transition. We describe three types of distributions:

  • **GlobalPixelTemporalTransformation DS**: represents the temporal variation of the pixels intensity on the full frame during the transition.
  • **TemporalDistributionRegion DS**: represents a shape and its temporal position. It describes, for example, a fade where the new video segment

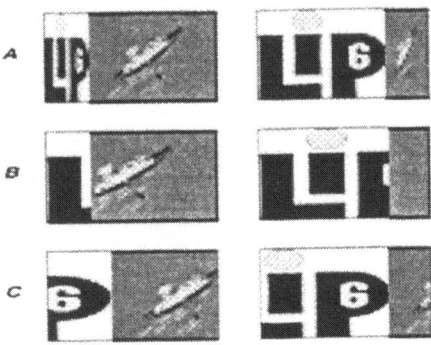

Figure 3. A represents a wipe where the frames are mapped on the mask. In B, the frames are masked and in C, they are tracked creating a wipe called push.

appears on little squares. Squares are randomly distributed over the previous video segment frames during the transition.

- **Foreground/Background-TransitionTemporalMask DSs**: These DSs represent the masks where the frames of next or previous shots appear or disappear (TransitionTemporalMask). As said, these masks are described like a video document (TemporalMaskFile), like a shape changing in the time (TemporalMask DS based on other DS of MPEG-7), or as a reference to a complementary mask (ComplementTemporalMask).

– **Foreground/Background-Transformation DSs**: These describe 3-D transformations applied to the frames of the background and foreground video segments. These DSs (3DTransformation) enable one to create transitions such as "page rolling".

Nowadays, digital editing products propose a considerable number of effects. We provide the DSs of four types of transition effects: cuts, fades, wipes and a generic class called special effects. DSs of other transitions can be easily developed by inheritance of TransitionType or GradualTransition DS.

10.6. Cut and Fade DSs

Cut is an abrupt transition. The DS used to describe this transition comes from TransitionType DS and fixes its duration to zero.

The DS called fade is a gradual transition type. It comes from Gradual Transition DS, and two particular DSs among its DistributionType DSs will be used: the GlobalPixelTemporalTransformation DS and the Temporal DistributionRegion DS. All types of fades can be built using this DS. Transitions such as "water drops" (this effect simulates how the water surface moves after the fall of a drop) may be created using the 3DTransformation DS (Foreground-/Background-Transformation) of the GradualTransition DS. We have added an analytic descriptor to highlight the difference between fades and other gradual effects: the CombinationType. This descriptor will be used for applications which do not need to re-build the editing work but need only the description of it. The CombinationType D allows us to specify the fade type (CombType D: fade in, fade out or cross-dissolve) and the color used for the fades in or out.

10.7. Wipe DS

The wipe is also a gradual effect and its DS comes from GradualTransition DS. As in the Fade DS, we propose analytic descriptors to replace more detailed ones used in the GradualTransition DS, in particular, those provided by the DistributionType DS:

– **FrameMotionActivity D**: indicates the presence of frame motion. This is not a motion within the frames of both sequences, but a motion of the full frames, as a scroll for example. If this motion exists, the D indicates which is the frame in motion. With this D, we can describe almost all the existing wipes. For example, for the effect frequently called "push", this D will take a value "all" (all in motion) because the frames of the next shot push the frames of the current shot.

    – **WipeMotion D**: represents the wipe motion direction with a motion vector. The wipe is characterized by the type of motion of the effect or of the frames (both in some cases).

10.8. Keyframe DS

This is one of the representative images of a shot. Keyframe DS inherits some other MPEG-7 DS that provides an ID and information about image content and annotations. The localization of the Keyframe file (URL) and the keyframe position in the video document (Time DS) are added

10.9. Shot DS

In our model a shot respects the already given definitions and comes from VideoSegment DS, other DS of the MDS (Multimedia Description Scheme) of MPEG-7. This inheritance provides pieces of information which are not linked with the editing work or which are semantic. They contain, for example, annotations and information about the dominant color, the camera motion, etc. As a minimum, a shot is identified with an identifier. Some descriptors give its localization and duration. This DS contains also the following information:

    – **ShotValidation D**: indicates if the shot is already validated. It is useful to resume the status of a validation process, which was stopped before the end of the video document.

    – **Sequence of Rush DSs**: is a group of rushes belonging to the same shot. They appear in the full frames eventually involved by video composition effects. For a classical shot without rush compositions, there is only one rush.

    – **Sequence of keyframes DSs**: is a group of representative images of a shot (keyframes). The number of selected keyframes may vary when a camera works or a composition rush takes place. They can belong to different rushes.

    – **Sequence of CompositionRush DSs**: is an ordered group of video composition rushes belonging to the same shot.

    – **Sequence of VideoCompositionEffects DSs**: is an ordered group of composition effects appearing in the same shot.

10.10. CompositionRush DS

This describes the composition of the rushes into a shot following the composition definition. It inherits from VideoSegment DS, including temporal segment localization and information about dominant color and motion, annotations, etc. Composition rush is described by a sequence of CompositionMask DSs, which define the frame regions where the different rushes will be edited. An example of composition is shown in Figure 4. These masks are similar to those used in the construction of gradual transition effects (Foreground/BackgroundTransition Temporal Mask DSs). They can be superimposed depending on their level (MaskLevel D).

10.10.1. CompositionMask DS

The compositionMask represents a frame region which is an element of a video composition. One or several rushes can appear in this mask. This mask can be seen as a spatial reduction of a video document where an editing work can be realized. So, this DS contains an EditionWorkIntraCompositionMask DS which describes the process. The CompositionMask DS contains the following elements:

– **CompositionTemporalMask DS**: as for the TransitionTemporalMask DS (see section 10.5), it describes the shape of the mask and its temporal evolution.

– **CompositionMaskLevel D**: gives the superimposition level of the masks. This level may change during the composition rush.

– **Transparency D**: is a matrix of transparency values for superimposed masks. This descriptor is optional because the mask can be described by a video document which already represents the transparency through its pixel values.

– **EditingWorkIntraCompositionMask DS**: this DS represents a sequence of rushes mapped on the mask and a sequence of internal transition effects (InternalTransitionEffect DS).

10.11. Rush DS

This DS describes rushes. It inherits from VideoSegment DS. VideoSegment provides information of the rush, independently with the described audiovisual

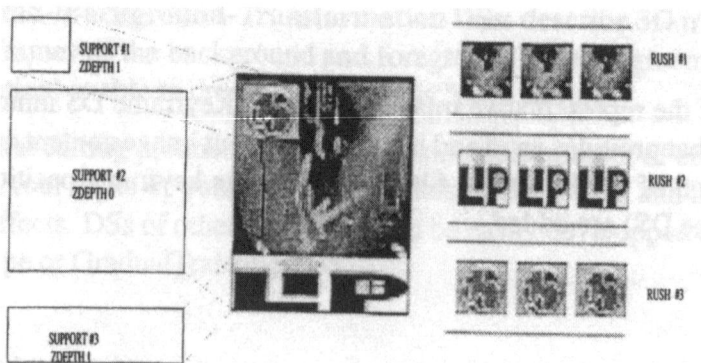

Figure 4. *The central image is a frame of a composition. The rushes present on the left part of the figure will be mapped on the masks, or masked by the masks present on the right part. The Rush#1 is masked and the others are mapped.*

(AV) document. It indicates if it is an image, a graphic, etc. For example, a rush can be formed by the logo of a TV channel or a particular TV program. To represent a rush formed by a text, as subtitles, we add a TextContent D. It provides the font, the style and the color of the text. It also indicates if the background is or not transparent and, ultimately, its color.

The localization of the rush in the final document is given by the TimeFinalCut DS.

The Rush DS provides the number of frames at the beginning and the end of the original rush (BeginningFrames/EndingFrames DS), that will be cut out to build the shot (see Figure 5).

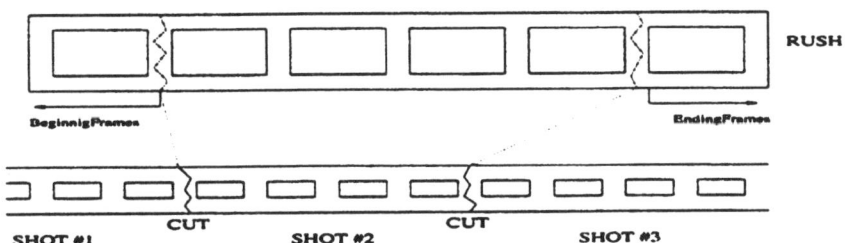

Figure 5. *A subpart of the rush will be taken to build the second shot*

11. Conclusions

The evolution of automatic segmentation algorithms will need accurate definitions of transition effects to clearly determine what are the elements that must be taken into account by the detection processes. More precisely, an objective comparison between different temporal video segmentation systems must be based on a simple but strict methodology. We proposed and tested for such a comparison, a process that can be split into the following steps: gathering a common corpus, producing a common reference segmentation, the automatic comparison of document segmentations, and defining an appropriate global quality criterion.

We propose a DS which can be used to describe the video content in relation to the editing work. This DS was born from the need to build a reference for the evaluation of video-to-shots segmentation methods.

This work has been inspired by the technical field of the video editing world. We tried to develop the previous concepts as close as possible to the actual work done during this step in the film industry. For example: to produce a wipe, different sets of masks are used to hide some parts of the photograms; rushes are actually the basic elements of the editing work, whereas shots are generally the only temporal unit used with usual descriptions. This particular approach provides some specific tools for the description that must be taken into account in addressing the needs of the audiovisual production industry.

The DS presented allows one to create Edit Decision Lists (EDL) to build movies from a set of rushes. This requires, of course, further work on how the soundtrack must be mixed with the pictures, and on how the user profile must be taken into account to produce the editing description. At the same time, the DS provides an analytical description of video documents from the point of view of the editing work, which does not exist in EDL standards such as [SMP 93].

REFERENCES

[AIG 94] AIGRAIN P., JOLY P., "The Automatic Real-time Analysis of Film Editing and Transition Effects and its Applications", *Computers and Graphics*, vol. 18, num. 1, 1994, p. 93–103.

[ARD 99] ARDIZZONE E., HACID M.-S., "A Knowledge Representation and Reasoning Support for Modeling and Querying Video Data", *11th IEEE International Conference on Tools with Artificial Intelligence,* 8–10 November, Chicago, Illinois, 1999.

[BEE 97] BEEFERMAN D., et al., "Text Segmentation Using Exponential Models", *Proc. Empirical Methods in Natural Language Processing 2, (AAAI'97)*, 1997.

[BOR 96] BORECZKY J., ROWE L., "Comparison of Video Boundary Detection Techniques", *Proceedings of SPIE*, vol. 2670, 1996, p. 170–179.

[COR 95] CORRIDONI J.M., DEL BIMBO A., "Film Semantic Analysis", *Proceedings of the International Conference on Analysis of Image Pattern*, vol. 3, 1995.

[DAI 95] DAILIANAS A., ALLEN R., ENGLAND P., "Comparison of Automatic Video Segmentation Algorithms", *Proc. SPIE. Photonics West,* Philadelphia, USA, October 1995.

[DAR 93] DARPA, *Proc. of DARPA Speech and Natural Language Workshop*, NIST, 1993.

[DAV 91] DAVENPORT G., SMITH T., PINCEVER N., "Cinematic Primitives for Multimedia", *IEEE Computer Graphics and Applications*, July, 1991, p. 67–74.

[EIC 00] EICKELER S., RIGOLL G., "A Novel Error Measure for the Evaluation of Video Indexing Systems", *Proceedings of ICASSP,* Istanbul, Turkey, June, 2000.

[GAR 88] GARY A.H., *Video Editing and Post-Production: A Professional Guide*, Knowledge Industry Publications, 1988.

[GOL 92] GOLIOT-LÉTÉ V.F.A., *Précis d'Analyse Filmique*, Cinema 128, Nathan University, 1992.

[GTI 99] GT-10 s., "French Working Group 10", 1999. *http://www.asim.lip6.fr/AIM/*

[HAM 94] HAMPAPUR A., JAIN R., WEYMOUTH T., "Digital Video Segmentation", *Proc. ACM Multimedia*, 1994, p. 357–564.

[HAM 95] HAMPAPUR A., JAIN R., WEYMOUTH T., "Production Model-based Digital Video Segmentation", *Multimedia Tools and Applications*, vol. 1, 1995, p. 9–46.

[HAU 98] HAUPTMANN A.G., WITBROK M.J., "Story Segmentation and Detection of Commercials In Broadcast News Video", *Advances in Digital Libraries Conference*, 1998.

[JOL 99] Joly P., et al., "Video Editing Work Description Scheme", *Proposal for MPEG-7 Meeting*, 1999.

[LUP 98] Lupatini G., Saraceno C., Leonardi R., "Scene Break Detection: A Comparison", *Proc. VIIIth Intern. Workshop on RIDE*, 1998, p. 34–41.

[MAR 99] Martínez J.M., "MPEG-7 Overview (version 1.0)", *ISO/IEC JTC1/SC29/WG11/ MPEG99/WG11/N3138 December 1999/Maui*, 1999.

[MPE 99] MPEG-7, "Description of MPEG-7 Content Set", *ISO-IEC JTC1/SC29/WG11/ N2467*, 1999.

[NAG 92] Nagasaka A., Tanaka Y., "Automatic Video Indexing and Full Video Search for Object Appearances", *IFIP Trans., Visual Database Systems II*, 1992, p. 113–128.

[RUI 99a] Ruiloba R., Joly P., et al., "An Analytic Description Scheme for Video Editing Work", *ISO/IEC JTC1/SC29/M5346 December 1999/Maui*, 1999.

[RUI 99b] Ruiloba R., Joly P., Marchand-Maillet S., Quénot G., "Towards a Standard Protocol for the Evaluation of Video-to-Shots Segmentation Algorithms", *Proceedings of International Workshop of CBMI,* Toulouse, France, 1999.

[RUI 00] Ruiloba R., et al., "A Description Scheme for Video Editing Work", *ISO/IEC JTC1/SC29/WG11/M5714 March 2000/Holland*, 2000.

[SMP 93] SMPTE, "SMPTE Standard for Television. Transfer of Edit Decision Lists. ANSI/SMPTE 258M–1993", *American National Standard/SMPTE Standard.* Approved February 5, 1993, p. 1–36.

[UED 91] Ueda H., Miyatake T., Yoshizawa S., "IMPACT: An Interactive Natural-Motion-Picture Dedicated Multimedia Authoring System", *INTERCHI'91, ACM*, 1991, p. 343–350.

[WOL 95] Wolf M.Y.B.–L.Y.W., Liu B., "Video Browsing using Clustering and Scene Transitions on Compressed Sequences", *SPIE Proc. on Multimedia Computing and Networking*, vol. 2417, 1995, p. 399–413.

[ZHA 93] Zhang H., Kankanhalli A., Smoliar S., "Automatic Partitioning of Full-Motion Video", *Multimedia Systems*, vol. 1, num. 1, 1993, p. 10–28.

Chapter 5

Real-time synchronization of distributed multimedia applications

Samar Mouchawrab
Nortel Networks, Ville Saint Laurent, Canada

Jocelyn Desbiens
INRS – Télécommunications, Montreal, Canada

1. Introduction

A distributed application is defined as a set of *n* processes $\{P_1, P_2,..., P_n\}$ running on physically separated processors. Three types of events occur in a process: *sending messages, delivering messages*, and *internal events*. Internal events act on the local variables only; they have no effects on the execution of the other processes. Sending and delivering message events represent the communication between processes of the distributed application. They have an important impact on the execution of the application, so their execution order must be respected.

Unreliable networks, and delays produced by asynchronous networks on the delivery of a message, may cause a message loss or a change of ordering. To solve this problem, a relationship, called *causal order*, is defined between events. This relationship is based on Lamport's Happened-Before relation, noted $\rightarrow$. Algorithms implementing causal order ensure a correct ordering of events using control information transmitted within messages. In practice, a number of *ordering semantics* for supporting synchronization are defined in the literature, such as total ordering, source (local) ordering, partial ordering, causal ordering, section ordering, attribute ordering and associate hybrid ordering [HAD 93].

In addition to the order of events, each message has a *lifetime* Δ. The lifetime of a message is the physical time duration, after its sending time, during which such a message can be used by its destination process. If a message arrives at its destination after its lifetime then it is discarded; for target processes such messages are actually lost. Otherwise, it is delivered at the target process within the expiration of its lifetime. In multimedia systems, the lifetime of a message is the maximum transmission delay that an application can tolerate before delivering a message before the quality of its service degrades.

Another relationship between events, the Δ-causal order, has been defined to deal with the lifetime of messages. In the previous algorithms implementing the Δ-causal order, the postulate is that Δ has a fixed constant value. In practice, the lifetime of a message is a function of its type and its priority. For instance, an audio or a video message has a different lifetime than a text or an advertisement message.

In a large multimedia distributed application running on the Internet, there is a need to synchronize audio and video streams as well as events carrying coordinates of objects or characters traveling in the application's virtual world. Events synchronization provides users with a good quality of service and is mandatory in cases such as a real-time distributed application.

The rest of the paper is structured as follows: Section 2 describes synchronization mechanisms and gives an example of the synchronization in multimedia applications. Section 3 contains formal definition of causal and Δ-causal orders as well as some other definitions. Section 4 describes previous work and algorithms implementing causal and Δ-causal orders. In Section 5, we present an example of Δ-causal order with variable Δ. We give our algorithm in Section 6 and its proof of correctness in Section 7. Section 8 is concerned with benchmarks obtained from an implementation of the algorithm. We conclude in Section 9.

2. Multimedia and synchronization

Multimedia synchronization refers to the maintenance of real-time constraints across more than one media type. It is a complex task and is mainly concerned with arbitrary real-time relationships between different interactions, whether discrete or continuous. The involved synchronization mechanisms must operate without failure in a distributed environment, potentially involving both LAN and WAN topologies irrespective of the location of the objects involved in the applications. Examples of intermedia synchronization include lip synchronization between audio and video channels [BLA 98], synchronization of text subtitles and video sequences, and synchronization mechanism of automatic simultaneous translation.

2.1. An example

The last decade has seen much progress in performance of speech recognition systems from cumbersome small vocabulary isolated word systems to large vocabulary continuous speech recognition over essentially unlimited vocabularies (100,000 words and more). Similarly, spoken language understanding systems now exist that process spontaneously spoken queries, although only in limited task domains under benign recording conditions (high quality, single speaker, no noise). It is not presumptuous to envision that, in a foreseeable future, automatic tools to perform simultaneous translation will be widely available and will replace the actual costly human translation systems. Such a system is pictured in Figure 1.

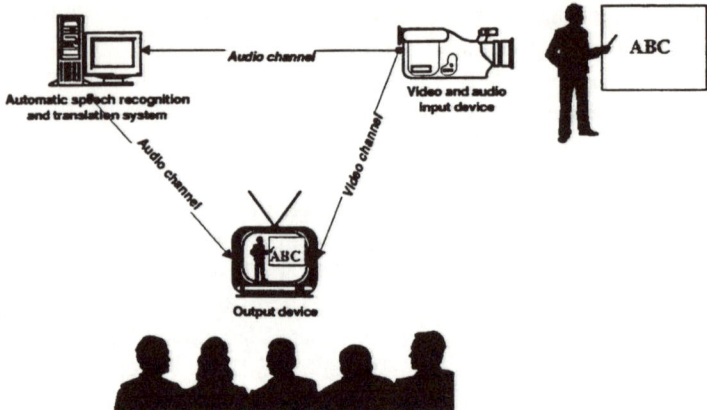

Figure 1. *An automatic simultaneous translation system*

The diagram shows an audio and video producer (a video camera), an audio only consumer (the speech recognition and automatic translation system or *translator*), and a video and audio consumer (the TV set). These are connected by appropriate audio and video stream channels. It is obvious from the QoS standpoint that the data coming from the video stream must be synchronized with the translated data being generated on the audio stream. Typical QoS constraints that must be met by such a system are:

 – a video channel offering a throughput of 25 frames per second, a delay of between 40 and 60 ms, and a frame lifetime of 20 ms;
 – an audio channel offering a throughput of 5 packets per second, a delay of between 40 and 60 ms, and a packet lifetime of 100 ms;
 – an automatic translation system adding an average delay of 20 ms per audio packet processed.

Synchronization of multimedia events can either be expressed in absolute terms with respect to a global real-time clock or, in the case of distributed applications missing a global clock, in relative terms with respect to each other. This is the kind of synchronization style that will be used throughout the paper. An example is depicted in Figure 2.

3. Definitions

The Happened-Before relation is defined in [LAM 78] as follows:

Definition 1. *Given two events a and b, we say that a* happened before *b, noted a* → *b, if at least one of the following conditions is satisfied:*

 – *a and b are two events of the same process, a occurs before b;*

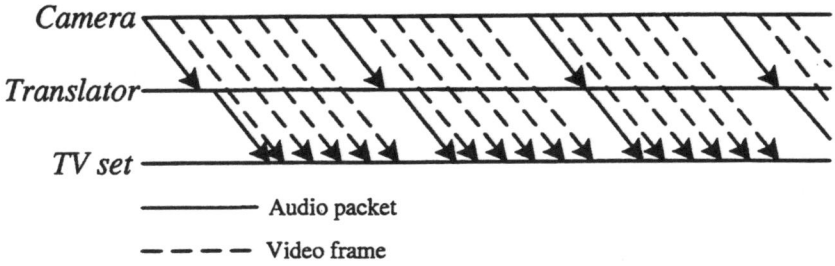

Figure 2. Synchronization of multimedia events

  – $a =$ **send**(m) *the event of sending a message m, and b =* **deliver**(m) *the event of delivering the same message m;*
  – *there is an event c with $a \rightarrow c$ and $c \rightarrow b$.*

We say that a and b are *concurrent events* if ab and $b \nrightarrow a$.

The causal order is defined as a causal and effect relation between events.

Definition 2. *Two sending events are said to be* causally dependent *if m_1 and m_2 have the same destination P_i and if* **send**$(m_1) \rightarrow$ **send**(m_2) *then* **deliver**$_p i$ $(m_1) \rightarrow$ **deliver**$_p i$ (m_2). *Furthermore, in the Δ-causal order, messages must be delivered within their lifetime.*

Definition 3. *We say that the event a is the* direct predecessor at process P_i, *of event b, noted $a \rightarrow_i b$, if a is the last event created in P_i that causally precedes b:*

  – $a \rightarrow b$, *a is created by P_i, and*
  – *if c is an event created by P_i and $c \rightarrow b$, then $c \rightarrow a$.*

To preserve causal order, a message m carries information about the direct predecessors of **send**(m) (from all processes) which are events of sending messages to the same destination as m. This set of events is called the *causal barrier* and is used to control information in the algorithm implementing the Δ-causal order. We note by **CB**(m) the causal barrier of the sending event of m (see Figure 3).

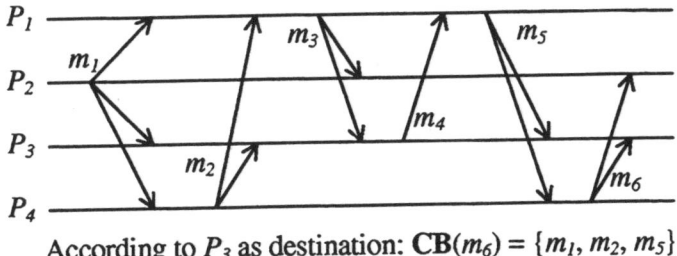

According to P_3 as destination: **CB**$(m_6) = \{m_1, m_2, m_5\}$

Figure 3. Example of causal barrier

In some implementations, the direct predecessor of an event b does not correspond to a process. If a is a direct predecessor of b then $a \rightarrow b$, and there is no event c such that: $a \rightarrow c \rightarrow b$. The causal barrier of b in these implementations corresponds to the concurrent messages causally preceding b. These definitions do not work well with variable message lifetime. In conclusion, we have adopted Definition 3 above.

4. Previous works

One of the objectives of algorithms implementing the causal and Δ-causal orders is to reduce the global amount of control information, which is the main source of communication overhead.

Vector clocks [MAR 93] are one of the mechanisms used to ensure causal order. They were implemented in many algorithms of causal ordering [ACH 92, BIR 91, RAY 91, SIN 92]. These algorithms have no real-time delivery constraint. In [BAL 96a], the Δ-causal order has been implemented to cope with temporal constraint. Each message carries a $n \times n$ matrix of time-stamps of the last messages communicated between processes. For special cases, where a chain of dependencies between events cannot have length greater than two, the Δ-causal order have been verified in [ADE 95] using the triangle inequality. This algorithm has linear order.

As a mean to reduce the volume of control information, causal barrier defined as the set of concurrent direct predecessor of an event is used in [BAL 96b] to implement an algorithm of Δ-causal order for broadcast communications. This concept of causal barrier has been used also in [PRA 97] to implement an efficient algorithm of causal ordering. This algorithm does not require any prior knowledge of the network topology or communication pattern. It has $O(n^2)$ order in the worst case, and has linear order in case of broadcast.

In order to avoid the full complexity of the whole problem, all known Δ-causal order implementations assume a unique lifetime for all messages. In case of types of messages with different lifetimes, the minimum among them is assumed as the unique lifetime to be respected by all messages. This paper gives the first complete implementation of the Δ-causal order with variable Δ.

5. Example of communication with variable Δ

In this section, we give an example of communication showing the problems that the different lifetimes of messages could cause.

The time-stamp (*sender_id, send_time, lifetime*) uniquely identifies the message M transmitted by the process $P_{sender-id}$ at the global time *send_time*. To reduce control information, each message carries a causal barrier related to all processes in the application as defined in Section 3. In Figure 4, the following dependency chain is identified: **send**$(M_x) \rightarrow$ **send**$(M_y) \rightarrow$ **send**$(M^l) \rightarrow$ **send**(M). M carries information about M_y in its causal barrier according to P_k, because it is the

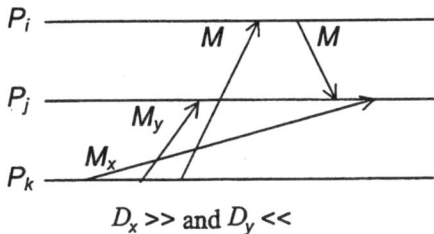

Figure 4. *Example of communication with variable* Δ

last message transmitted by P_k to P_j, the destination of M. This information is passed from M^l to P_i who sends M.

Suppose that M_y expires before M_x, ($send\_time_{Mx} + \Delta_x > send\_time_{My} + \Delta_y$). If M is received at P_j before the reception of M_x and M_y, it waits for the delivery or the expiration of messages in its causal barrier (M_y) to insure Δ-causal order. So M can be delivered after the expiration of M_y and before the delivery of M_x. Thus, at the delivery of M_x after the delivery of M, the causal order will be violated. In order not to violate causal ordering with M_x, M cannot be delivered even if M_y expires. Thus the time-stamp of M_y in the causal barrier of M must contain a parameter T indicating the last instant of expiration of messages transmitted by P_k that causally precede M. In this case, $T = \max(send\_time_{Mx} + \Delta_x, send\_time_{My} + \Delta_y)$. M waits for the delivery of M_y or the expiration of T to be delivered.

If $send\_time_M + \Delta_M < T$, then M could expire before the reception of M_x. In order to not violate the causal order, M must be discarded at the end of its lifetime if M_x is not received, but M_x could be lost at this point, thus no message will be delivered to P_k, even M which has been received and expired before the reception of its predecessors. Consequently, we decided that messages received at their destinations and waiting for their predecessors to be delivered, must be delivered at the end of their lifetimes in the case that their predecessors have not been received, even if they are not expired. In this case M does not wait for the expiration of T to be sure that all causally precedent messages have expired, it will be delivered at the limit of its lifetime ($send\_time_M + \Delta_M$), and undelivered messages in its causal barrier will be added to a set of discarded messages, *Discarded*. Thus, if M_x arrives at P_j after the delivery of M, it will be discarded because it is an element of the set *Discarded*.

6. Algorithms and data structures

Each message M has a group of destination processes represented by an integer set, *destination(M)*. Each element of *destination(M)* represents the identity of one of the destination processes of M. The sending time of M is the current global time, *current_time*, at the moment of sending M. Each process P_i maintains three variables

Algorithm 1.

function send(M, P_i, P_j) : **nil**;
{This function sends a message M from P_i to P_j. No values are returned.}

begin {send algorithm}
1. $sent_i := current\_time$;
2. **forall** $P_j \in destination(M)$ **do** send $(M, i, sent_i, \Delta_M, destination(M), \mathbf{CB}_i)$ to P_j;
3. **forall** $P_j \in destination(M)$ **do** $\mathbf{CB}_i[j] := \mathbf{CB}_i[j] \cup_{max T} \{(i, sent_i, \Delta_M, sent_i + \Delta_M)\}$
end{send algorithm}.

Algorithm 2.

function receive$(M, j, sent_M, \Delta_M, destination(M), \mathbf{CB}_M)$: **nil**;
{This functions receives a message $(M, j, sent_M, \Delta_M, destination(M), \mathbf{CB}_M)$ from P_j.
No values are returned.}

begin {receive algorithm}
1. **if** $(sent_M + \Delta_M < current\_time) \vee ((j, sent_M, \Delta_M) \in Discarded_i)$
2. **then** discard M
3. **else**
4. **begin**
5.   **wait until**
6.   **forall** $P_k \in \{P_l \mid (l, x, \Delta_x, T_x) \in \mathbf{CB}_M[i]\}$ **do**
7. $(Delivered_i[k, i] \geq x) \vee ((k, x, \Delta_x) \in Discarded_i) \vee (current\_time > T_x))$
8. $\vee (sent_M + \Delta_M \leq current\_time)$;
9.   **forall** $P_k \in \{P_l \mid (l, x, \Delta_x, T_x) \in \mathbf{CB}_M[i]\}$ **do**
10.   **if** $(Delivered_i[k, i] < x) \wedge ((k, x, \Delta_x) \notin Discarded_i) \wedge (current\_time < T_x)$
11.   **then** $Discarded_i := Discarded_i \cup_{max T} \{(k, x, \Delta_x, T_x)\}$;
12.   deliver M;
13. $Delivered_i[j, i] := sent_M$;
14.   **forall** $1 \leq k \leq n$ **do if** $(k, y, \Delta_y, T_y) \in \mathbf{CB}_M[j]$ **then** $Delivered_i[k, j] := \max(Delivered_i[k, j], y)$;
15.   **forall** $k \in destination(M)$ **do** $\mathbf{CB}_i[k] := \mathbf{CB}_i[k] \cup_{max T} \{(j, sent_M, \Delta_M, sent_M + \Delta_M)\}$;
16.   **forall** $1 \leq k \leq n$ **do** $\mathbf{CB}_i[k] := \mathbf{CB}_i[k] \cup_{max T} \mathbf{CB}_M[k]$;
17. $\mathbf{CB}_i[j] := \mathbf{CB}_i[j] \setminus_{max} \mathbf{CB}_M[j]$;
18.   **forall** $1 \leq k \leq n, k \neq i$ **do**
19.   **forall** $(l, x, \Delta_x, T_x) \in \mathbf{CB}_i[k]$ **do**
20.   **if** $(Delivered_i[l, k] \geq x) \vee (current\_time > T_x)$ **then** $\mathbf{CB}_i[k] := \mathbf{CB}_i[k] \setminus \{(l, x, \Delta_x, T_x)\}$;
21.   **forall** $(k, x, \Delta_x, T_x) \in Discarded_i$ **do**
22.   **if** $(current\_time > T_x)$ **then** $Discarded_i := Discarded_i \setminus \{(k, x, \Delta_x, T_x)\}$
23. **end**;
end{receive algorithm}.

used in the algorithm of Δ-causal order and represents the control information. These variables are: $\mathbf{CB}_i$, $Delivered_i$ and $Discarded_i$:

– $\mathbf{CB}_i$ is a vector of length n, where n is the number of processes in the distributed application. Each element of $\mathbf{CB}_i$, of maximum length $n - 1$, is a set of tuples of the form (*sender_id, sending_time*, Δ, T) called *time-stamps*. $\mathbf{CB}_i[j]$, for $j \neq i$, represents the causal barrier of the future message to send from P_i to P_j. And $\mathbf{CB}_i[i]$ represents the set of the most recent messages delivered to P_i from the other processes, one message per process;

– *Delivered_i* is a $n \times n$ matrix of time, representing the P_i's knowledge of the most recent messages delivered to the other processes. If *Delivered_i*[j, k] = t, then P_i knows that the message transmitted by P_j to P_k at time t has been delivered to P_k and all messages transmitted by P_j to P_k before t have been delivered, expired, or discarded;

– *Discarded*$_i$ is a set of time-stamps. It contains at most $n - 1$ elements. If $(j, t, \Delta, T) \in$ *Discarded*$_i$ then every message received at P_i from P_j transmitted before or at t must be discarded.

Our algorithm consists of two functions: send a message and receive a message (see Algorithms 1 and 2). In these functions, the meaning of the operations $\in$, $\cup_{max\,T}$, and $\backslash_{max\,T}$ is as follows:

– $(i, x, \Delta_x) \in$ *Discarded*$_j$ if there is $(l, y, \Delta_y, T_y) \in$ *Discarded*$_j$, where $(i = l, x = y,$ and $\Delta_x = \Delta_y)$ or $(i = l,$ and $x < y)$;

– $A := A_1 \cup_{max\,T} A_2 \Rightarrow A$ is the result of replacing each existing pair of time-stamps (i, x, Δ_x, T_x) and (i, y, Δ_y, T_y) in $A_1 \cup A_2$ with the time-stamp (i, z, Δ_z, T_x), where $z := \max(x, y)$, $\Delta_x := \Delta_{\max(x, y)}$, and $T_x := \max(T_x, T_y)$;

– $A := A_1 \backslash_{max\,T} A_2 \Rightarrow A$ is the result of removing from A_1 the time-stamps (i, x, Δ_x, T_x), where there is $(i, y, \Delta_y, T_y) \in A_2$ with $x \leq y$.

The control information to send within a message (causal barrier) is of order $O(n^2)$, where n is the number of processes in the application. Not all elements of the causal barrier matrix contain information, thus there can be a reduction of the size of control information. Actually, the order of the algorithm is $O(n^2)$ in the worst case.

7. Proof of correctness

To show safety and functionality of our algorithm (Theorems 1, 2 and 3), we prove first the following three Lemmas.

Lemma 1. *Let M_x and M be two messages to destination P_j, where P_k sends M_x to P_j, P_i sends M to P_j, and M_x is identified by (k, x, Δ_x). If $(k, x, \Delta_x, T_x) \in CB_M[j]$ then* send $(M_x) \rightarrow$ send (M).

Proof. $CB_M[j]$ is a copy of $CB_i[j]$ before P_i sends M, thus $(k, x, \Delta_x, T_x) \in CB_i[j]$. This time-stamp might be added to $CB_i[j]$ at step 3 of Algorithm 1, thus $k = i$ and send $(M_x) \rightarrow$ send (M) because (M_x) happened before M. (k, x, Δ_x, T_x) might be also added at step 15, therefore (M_x) is sent and delivered to P_i before it sends M, send $(M_x) \rightarrow$ deliver $P_i (M_x) \rightarrow$ send (M). Also, (k, x, Δ_x, T_x) might be added at step 16, thus there exists a message M' sent by P_i to P_i that causally depends on (M_x). M' passes (k, x, Δ_x, T_x) from its causal barrier to P_i. Or $(k, x, \Delta_x, T_x) \in CB_i[j] \downarrow (k, x, \Delta_x, T_x)$ has been added to $CB_i[j]$ at steps 3, 15 or 16 as above. We conclude that there exist a chain of dependency send $(M_x) \rightarrow \cdots \rightarrow$ send (M).

Lemma 2. *If there is a dependency chain:* send $(M_1) \rightarrow \cdots \rightarrow$ send (M_n), *where P_k sends M_1 to P_i, P_i sends M_n to P_j, and M_1 is identified by $(k, \text{sent}_1, \Delta_1)$, and if we stop the deletion of time-stamps from causal barriers in the algorithms 1 and 2, then $\exists T$ such that $(k, \text{sent}_1, \Delta_1, T) \in CB_{Mn}[j]$.*

Proof. Let $C_{pl'}$ = chain of deliver and send events within P_l, and

$$C_{sdpl} = \text{send}_{Pm} \rightarrow \text{deliver}_{Pl}(M) \rightarrow C_{Pl'}^*,$$

where P_m is the process that causes the event before *send(M)*. Thus we have

$$\text{send}_{Pk} \rightarrow_{Pj} (M_1) \rightarrow C_{Pj}^* \rightarrow C_{sdpl}^* \rightarrow C_{sdpi}^* \rightarrow \text{send}_{Pi} \rightarrow_{Pj} (M_n),$$

and $(k, sent_1, \Delta_1, T_1) \in \mathbf{CB}_{k[j]}$ (step 3 of Algorithm 1). When getting from P_m to P_l, $(k, sent_1, \Delta_1, T_1)$ is added to $\mathbf{CB}_l[j]$ (step 16 of Algorithm 2). Within a C_{Pl}, chain, $(k, sent_1, \Delta_1, T_1)$ is kept in $\mathbf{CB}_l[j]$ (hypothesis of Lemma 2). Thus $(k, sent_1, \Delta_1, T_1)$ passes through the chain to $\mathbf{CB}_{Mn}[j]$.

Lemma 3. *Let M_x and M be two messages with the same destination P_j. Assume that P_k sends M_x to P_j, P_i sends M to P_j, and M_x is identified by (k, x, Δ_x). If*

1. **send** $(M_x) \rightarrow$ **send** (M),
2. **deliver** $_{Pj}(M_x) \not\rightarrow$ **send** (M),
3. *there is no M_y such that P_k sends M_y to P_j, where* **send** $(M_x) \rightarrow$ **send** $(M_y) \rightarrow$ **send** (M), *and*
4. *(M_x) has not expired before P_i sends M to Pj, and*
5. *$(k, x, \Delta_x) \notin Discarded_j$,*
then $\exists T$ such that $(k, x, \Delta_x, T) \in \mathbf{CB}_M[j]$.

Proof. Since there is a dependency chain between **send** (M_x) and **send** (M), the time-stamp can be deleted before arriving to $\mathbf{CB}_M[j]$ at step 3 of Algorithm 1 or steps 15, 16, 17 and 20 of Algorithm 2. At step 3, the deletion is caused by a message M_y sent after M_x by P_k to P_j. **send** (M_y) can't be part of the chain because **send**$(M_x) \rightarrow$ **send**$(M_y) \rightarrow$ **send**(M) violates the hypothesis 3. Then **send** (M_y) is outside the chain and the time-stamp of M_x hasn't been deleted. At steps 15, 16, 17 and 20, a message M_y sent by P_m and received by P_l is part of the dependency chain. At step 15, if $\mathbf{CB}_{My}$ causes the deletion of the time-stamp of M_x then $m = k$ (violation of hypothesis 3). At step 16, the deletion of the time-stamp of M_x implies that there is a message M_x in the same dependency chain, sent by P_k to P_J after M_x (violation of hypothesis 3). If the time-stamp of M_x is deleted at step 17, then M_y has P_j as destination $(m = j)$ and there is a message M_x sent by P_k to P_j after M_x in the same destination chain. The time-stamp of M_x has been deleted because $\mathbf{CB}_{My}[j]$ contains the time-stamp of M_z, which is more recent than the time-stamp of M_x. Or $\mathbf{CB}_{My}[j]$ is a copy of $\mathbf{CB}_m[j] = \mathbf{CB}_m[j]$ that represents the latest messages delivered to P_j. Thus, three cases can be considered: first, M_x has been delivered to P_j, (violation of hypothesis 2), second, M_x has expired (violation of hypothesis 4), third, M_x has been discarded (violation of hypothesis 5). Two cases can be again considered if (k, x, Δ_x, T_x) is deleted at step 20. First, $Delivered_j [k, j] \geq x$ then M_x has been delivered to P_j, (violation of hypothesis 2), or M_x has expired (violation of hypothesis 4), or M_x has been discarded (violation of hypothesis 5). Second, $T_x <$ current–time, thus M_x has expired (violation of hypothesis 4). We conclude that, with the hypothesis of Lemma 3, $\exists T$ such that $(k, x, \Delta_x, T) \in \mathbf{CB}_M [j]$

Theorem 1. *Algorithms 1 and 2 insure causal order.*

Proof. Let M_x and M be two messages sent to P_j under the same hypothesis as of Lemma 3. According to Lemmas 1, 2 and 3, $\exists T$ such that $(k, x, \Delta_x, T) \in \mathbf{CB}_M[j]$. If

P_j receives M before M_x, and if M does not expire before M_x, M will not be delivered until M_x is either delivered, expired or discarded (step 7 of Algorithm 2). If M expires before receiving M_x, M is delivered as soon as it expires. Consequently M_x is added to $Discarded_j$, and M_x will be discarded when received at P_j. We conclude that Algorithms 1 and 2 ensure the causal order between directly causal dependent messages having the same destination. Transitivity of happened-before relationship enforces the causal order for all messages of the application.

Theorem 2. *An expired message will never be delivered.*

Proof. Upon receiving an expired message, it will be discarded at step 2 of Algorithm 2. Thus no expired message can be delivered.

Theorem 3. *Always, a message eventually arriving to its destination before expiring is delivered.*

Proof. Let M be a message received by P_i. If M has not yet expired and is not an element of $Discarded_i$, then it will wait for messages in its causal barrier to be either delivered, expired or discarded, or for its lifetime to expire. When one of these two conditions is satisfied, M is delivered. If the time-stamp of M is an element of $Discarded_i$, then it will be discarded. This means that there was another message M' that causally followed M, has arrived to P_i before M, and is delivered because its lifetime has expired. Messages preceding M' will be discarded when received, but those following M' must be delivered, if not expired, when received until there is a message M'' following them that has been delivered at the upper limit of its lifetime (see Figure 5). Thus, always, there is a message received and delivered at P_i within the boundary of its lifetime. This theorem insures liveness property of Algorithms 1 and 2.

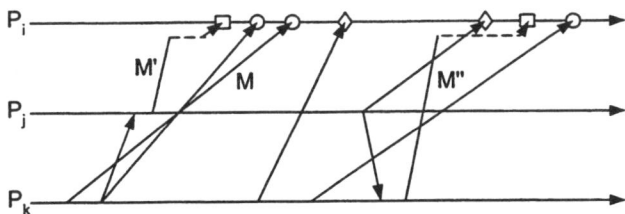

□ Message delivered at the limit of its lifetime without waiting messages in its causal barrier.

◇ Message delivered after messages in its causal barrier have been delivered, expired or discarded.

○ Message discarded.

Figure 5. Example of communication showing the liveness property of the algorithm

8. Performance evaluation

A simulation model has been developed in order to evaluate the performance of the proposed algorithm. The model consists of a distributed application of N processes running on P different processors. Different processes communicate between each other using sockets. A process can specify the set of destination processes of a message as well as its lifetime and its data size. Simulation experiments showed that after 300 messages sent by each process, the algorithm reaches its stability in terms of average causal barrier size. Thus, the approach for the simulation experiments was to send at least 500 messages per process in each experiment.

The model was implemented in C++ and run over a cluster of Windows/NT workstations.

8.1. Impact of the application size

Simulations were performed with different numbers of processes, varying from 4 to 40. Messages used in this simulation have different lifetimes (500, 1000, 1500 and 2000 ms). Part *a* of Figure 6 shows the simulation results with one destination process per message and an intermessage generation time fixed to 200 ms.

The x-axis represents the number of processes in the distributed application and the y-axis represents the average size of message causal barriers (as a percentage of the theoretical maximum value which is N^2). Part *b* of Figure 6 shows the same simulation results where the y-axis presents the average of tuples in a causal barrier. As a result, the size of causal barrier to send within a message increases with the number of processes. When the number of processes exceeds 20, the function $n_t = f(N)$ becomes linear, where n_t is the number of tuples in a causal barrier. In a multicast communication, savings in terms of causal barriers size are about 75% in a 40 process application.

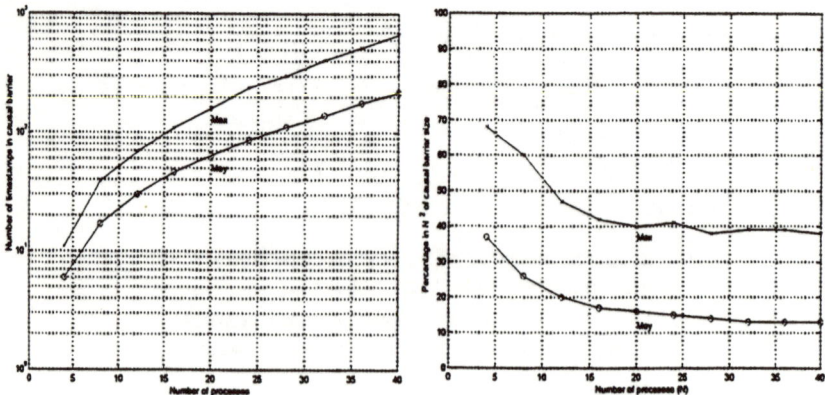

Figure 6. *Impact of the application size*

8.2. Impact of the number of destinations

For a 20 process application with messages of different lifetimes (500, 1000, 1500, and 2000 ms) and intermessage generation time fixed to 300 ms, the simulations were performed for number of destinations varying from 1 to 19. Figure 7 shows the simulation results where the x-axis represents the number of destinations for a message and the y-axis represents the average size of causal barriers as a percentage of N^2. The size of causal barriers increases with the number of destinations. It becomes constant for a communication when almost multicast.

8.3. Impact of data size

Varying the amount of data sent within a message has no impact on the size of causal barriers as shown by the simulation results of Figure 8. Simulations were performed on a distributed application of 15 processes and messages with different lifetimes and an intermessage generation time fixed to 500 ms.

8.4. Impact of message loss

Some protocols, such as UDP, do not guarantee the arrival of a message at its destination. This simulation intends to find out the impact of message loss on the amount of control information to be sent within a message. The simulation consists of a distributed application with 16 processes that communicate messages

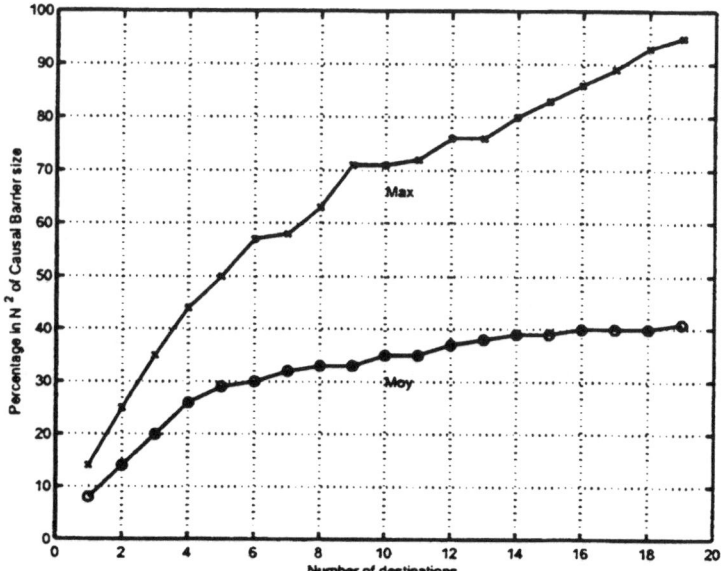

Figure 7. *Impact of number of destinations*

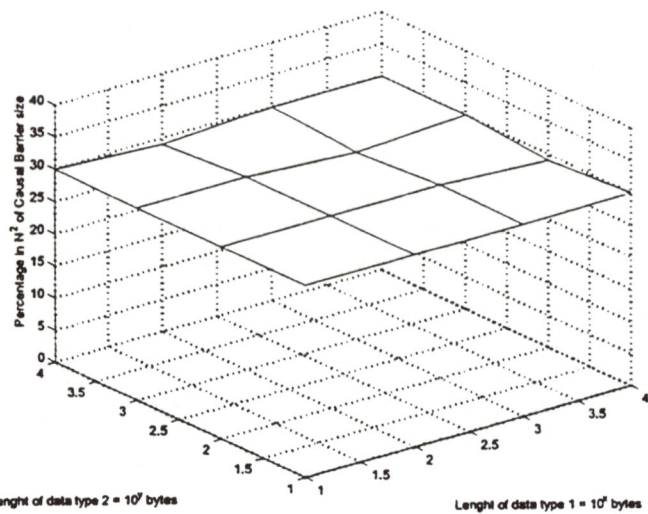

Figure 8. *Impact of data size*

of different lifetimes with an intermessage generation time fixed to 200 ms. Figure 9 shows the simulation results where the x-axis represents the probability of message lost varying from 0 to 100%. The size of causal barriers decreases when the probability of message loss increases. In general, this probability is kept low in order to ensure requirements in terms of quality of service. The results show that,

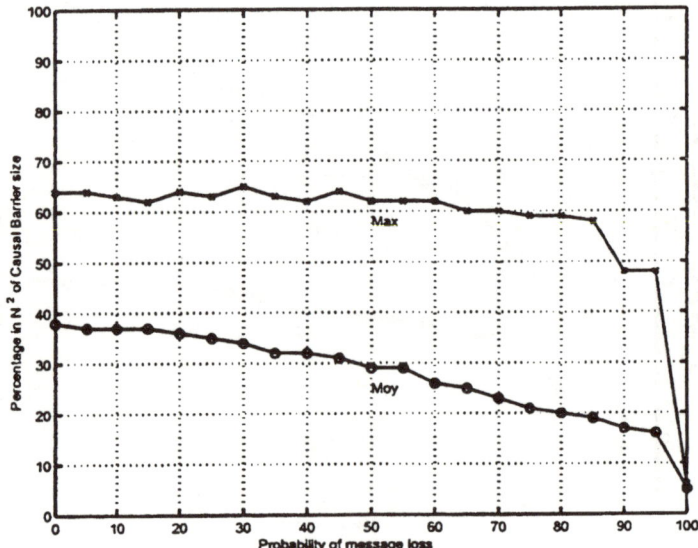

Figure 9. *Impact of message loss*

for lower probabilities, the size of causal barriers is almost constant. This means that the control information has not been lost even if there is message lost.

8.5. Impact of message delay

Network congestion problems, as well as routing problems, affect the end-to-end message delay. When a message arrives after its lifetime, control information – sent within this message – becomes useless. Thus, as shown in Figure 10, the amount of control information decreases when the probability of message delay increases.

8.6. Impact of message lifetime

Message lifetime has a significant impact on the size of causal barrier as can be inferred from Figure 11. The performance of the proposed algorithm was simulated for a system of 15 processes exchanging messages every 100 ms. Each message is sent to five different destinations with a loss probability of 10% and a delay probability of 10%.

Messages were of three types, each type corresponding to a different lifetime Δ_1, Δ_2, and Δ_3. In order to evaluate the impact of the lifetime of messages on the causal barrier size, 5 simulations were executed. In each simulation, Δ_1 was fixed, Δ_2, and Δ_3 varied from 100 ms to 1000 s. Results from Figure 11 show that:

– in each simulation, the minimal causal barrier size is obtained for $\Delta_1 = \Delta_2 = \Delta_3$. The minimal value obtained for all the simulation was for $\Delta_1 = \Delta_2 = \Delta_3 = 100$ ms;

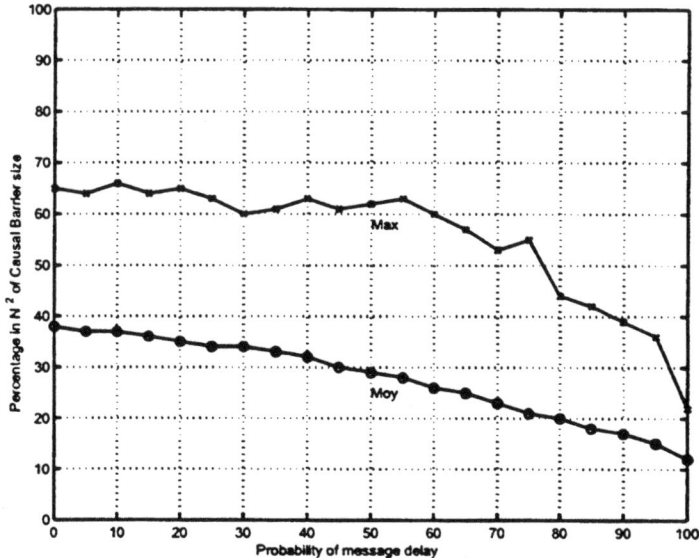

Figure 10. *Impact of message delay*

  – for $\Delta_2 = \Delta_3 = 10^4$ ms, the causal barrier size is greater when $\Delta_1 = 10^3$ ms than when $\Delta_1 = 10^4$ ms;

  – for $\Delta_2 = \Delta_3 = 1000$ s, the size of causal barrier increases when Δ_1 increases from 100 ms to 10^4 ms, then it decreases considerably for $\Delta_1 = 10^5$ ms and $\Delta_1 = 10^6$ ms.

As message lifetime increases, a process must wait longer for a message to be received before tagging it as lost or expired, thus more information must be kept in

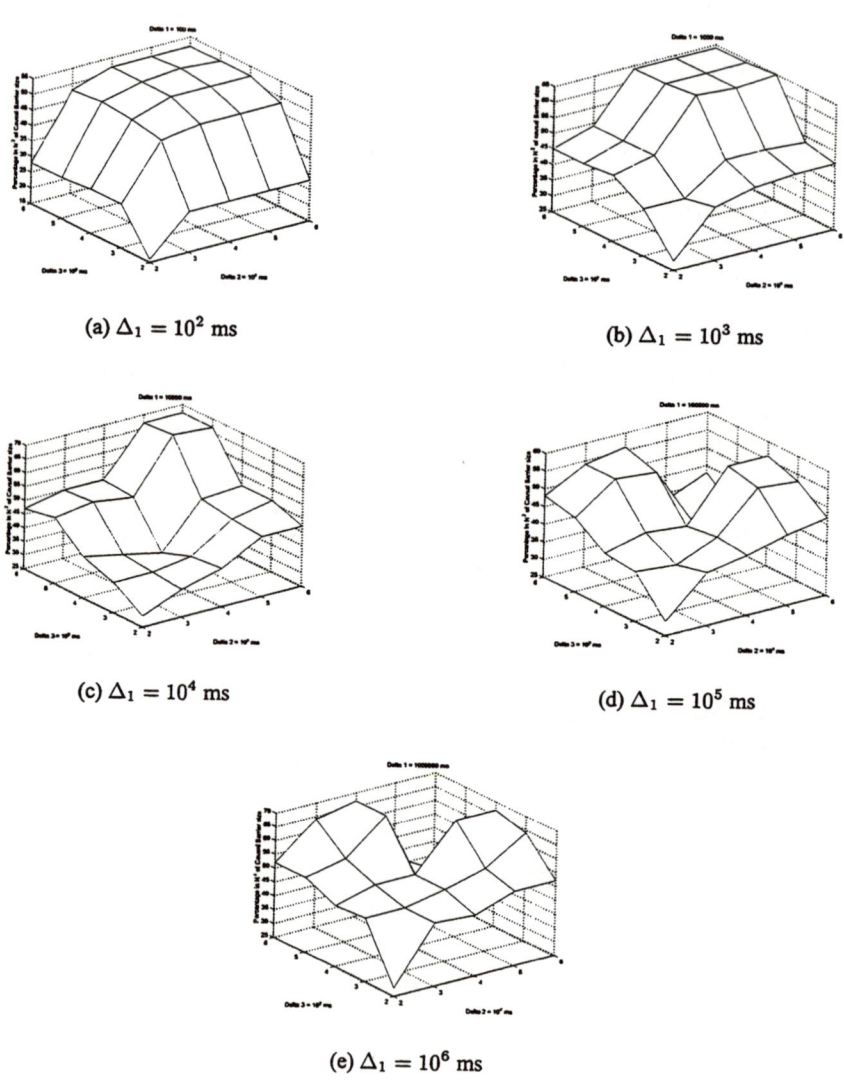

(a) $\Delta_1 = 10^2$ ms

(b) $\Delta_1 = 10^3$ ms

(c) $\Delta_1 = 10^4$ ms

(d) $\Delta_1 = 10^5$ ms

(e) $\Delta_1 = 10^6$ ms

Figure 11. *Impact of message lifetime*

causal barriers. Information about expired messages will be deleted from causal barriers more often in the case of shorter lifetimes than in the case of larger lifetimes.

In the case of messages with identical lifetimes, the size of a causal barrier is minimum due to the fact that there is no need to keep in the causal barrier information about predecessor messages of a delivered message; they must be delivered or expired.

In the case of messages with different lifetimes, predecessors of an expired message may not be yet expired. Thus, the greater the difference between message lifetimes, the more the information about expired messages must be kept in the causal barriers.

We conclude that causal barrier size increases when message lifetime increases, or when the difference between lifetimes increases.

9. Conclusion

We have built upon the existing algorithms of causal and Δ-causal orders with fixed Δ to develop a new Δ-causal order algorithm with variable message lifetime Δ. Our algorithm has a worst case complexity of $O(n^2)$. It is based on the concept of causal barrier, which greatly reduces control information and leads to a reduction in traffic overhead. We have implemented a distributed version of the algorithm (in C++ on Windows/NT platform) and shown some performance results we have obtained so far. In summary:

– the algorithm scales well, with savings in terms of causal barriers size of about 75% in a 40 processes application;
– is totally independent of the size and type of the data being transmitted;
– dynamically fits to new network topology;
– is stable regarding message loss and delay.

REFERENCES

[ACH 92] ACHARYA A., BADRINATH B., "Recording Distributed Snapshots Based on Causal Order of Message Delivery", *Information Processing Letters*, vol. 44, n° 6, 1992, p. 317–321.

[ADE 95] ADELSTEIN F., SINGHAL M., "Real-Time Causal Message Ordering in Multimedia Systems", *ICDCS*, 1995, p. 36–43.

[BAL 96a] BALDONI R., MOSTEFAOUI A., RAYNAL M., "Causal Delivery of Messages with Real-Time Data in Unreliable Networks", *Journal of Real-Time Systems*, vol. 10, n° 3, 1996.

[BAL 96b] BALDONI R., PRAKASH R., RAYNAL M., SINGHAL M., "Broadcast with Time and Causality Constraints for Multimedia Applications", *IEE EuroMicro Conference*, 1996, p. 617–624.

[BIR 91] Birman K., Schiper A., Stephenson P., "Lightweight Causal and Atomic Group Multicast", *ACM Transactions on Computer Systems*, vol. 9, n° 3, 1991, p. 272–314.

[BLA 98] Blair G., Stefani J., *Open Distributed Processing and Multimedia*, Addison-Wesley, Harlow, England, 1998.

[HAD 93] Hadzilacos V., Toueg S., *"Fault-tolerant Broadcasts and Related Problems"*, Addison-Wesley, Reading, MA, 1993.

[LAM 78] Lamport L., "Clocks and the Ordering of Events in a Distributed System", *Communications of the ACM*, vol. 21, n° 7, 1978, p. 558–565.

[MAR 93] Marzullo K., Babaoglu O., *"Consistent Global States of Distributed Systems: Fundamental Concepts and Mechanisms"*, Chapter 2, 1993.

[PRA 97] Prakash R., Raynal M., Singhal M., "An Adaptive Causal Ordering Algorithm Suited to Mobile Computing Environments", *Journal of Parallel and Distributed Computing*, vol. 41, 1997, p. 190–204.

[RAY 91] Raynal M., Schiper A., Toueg S., "The Causal Ordering Abstraction and a Simple Way to Implement It", *Information Processing Letters*, vol. 39, n° 6, 1991, p. 343–350.

[SIN 92] Singhal M., Kshemkalyani A., "An Efficient Implementation of Vector Clocks", *Information Processing Letters*, vol. 43, n° 1, 1992, p. 47–52.

Chapter 6

Active bandwidth sharing for multi-layered video in multi-source environments

Nadjib Achir and Guy Pujolle
Laboratoire LIP6 (CNRS – UPMC), Paris, France

Marcelo Dias de Amorim
Laboratoire LRI – UPS, Université Paris Sud, France

Otto Carlos M.B. Duarte
GTA – COPPE/EE – UFRJ, Rio de Janeiro, Brazil

1. Introduction

One of the greatest challenges of the last years is to provide large-scale video distribution with the required quality of service [LI 99, NON 99]. Dedicated networks and specific mechanisms have been introduced to allow the delivery of such strict applications with the best possible quality of service. Nevertheless, with the explosion of the Internet, new proposals have emerged to integrate video distribution in traditional best-effort networks. This integration offers many advantages including larger coverage, great flexibility, and reduced cost. But, several limitations can be identified like heterogeneity of receivers and scalability. New schemes must then be introduced to manage the transmission of the video streams in such a shared and unreliable environment [LI 99, AMO 00, SAP 00, RUB 99, SAR 00].

In the video system proposed in [AMO 00], each multicast tree is composed of one source that communicates periodically with a number of receivers. The exchanged information allows the source to calculate the rates of the video layers. The corresponding procedures form an adaptive control system that aims at optimizing the quality of the video at the receivers. With this architecture, the source sends a control packet that marks the available bandwidth, $C_s(l)$ in each traversed link l through the multicast tree. When a receiver r belonging to the multicast session m receives this packet, it computes the maximum rate it can receive,

$$b^{r,m} = \min_{l \in L_{s,r}} c_s(l),$$ [1]

where $L_s r$ is the set of links traversed by the control packet between the source s and the receiver r. The receiver builds then an acknowledgment packet containing this information and sends it back to the source. This mechanism optimizes the video quality in a way the source is aware about the receivers' capacities. However, this mechanism must be controlled to avoid scalability problems like feedback implosion at the source if the multicast session has a large number of receivers. In order to avoid this problem, nodes must implement a merging mechanism to reduce the load. This mechanism can be easily implemented if we have one multicast session. Unfortunately, if we consider a multi-source system where multiple multicast sessions share links in a network, other problems related to the bandwidth control and the quality of the video in the receivers must be solved. Where nodes experience congestion, a mechanism must act in order to decide which flows must be forwarded. From the point of view of the receivers, the node should prioritize the flows that it considers more important.

In order to achieve this target and to solve the fairness problems in the case of conflict among the receivers, we use the active network concept to provide a greater degree of fairness among the different flows. In our scheme, the receivers define an array where each entry i has two fields: the required multicast session, $m[sup]i_r$, and the priority assigned to this session, w_{mr}^i. We define a topology in order to analyze the behavior of one link traversed by different flows. The bandwidth is allocated to each flow in conformity with the priority assigned by the receivers to each required video. The results obtained show that the resource sharing is effective according to the priorities assigned to the flows. The system proves to be fair and fast, because it quickly provides the receivers with at least the base layer. Furthermore, the proposed scheme is efficient, attaining a bandwidth utilization of about 90% of the bottleneck link's capacity.

This article is organized as follows. In Section 2 we discuss the active network approach for the effective control of the video in the best-effort networks such as the Internet. Section 3 presents the problems and potential solutions. The analysis of the proposed model is detailed in Section 4. Finally, we present the conclusions in Section 5.

2. Video and active networks

Best-effort environments such as the Internet have some intrinsic characteristics for the deployment of applications requiring some level of quality of service. First, the receivers are heterogeneous in their data-handling capacities and the video quality required. Second, the available bandwidth of the links are variable. A good approach to face these limitations is the use of multi-layered video coding where each layer is transmitted in a different multicast tree. By conveying several video layers, the receivers can adjust the video quality by subscribing to different multicast groups. The larger the number of received video layers the better is the quality of the presentation. On the other hand, adhesion to a small number of multicast trees implies a worse quality but has the advantage of reduced allocated bandwidth. This method has the advantage of reduced interaction between the source and the receivers. Nevertheless, establishing multiple multicast trees means that a larger number of network states must be kept at the nodes.

We prove in this paper that the use of active networks is interesting for providing high performance and fairness in multi-source multicast video using the multi-layered approach. An active network allows intermediate nodes to perform tasks until now reserved for the application layer [WET 98, ALE 98, TEN 97, PSO 99, DEC 98]. Users can program the network by injecting their own codes in order to dynamically exploit the equipment of the network. The network then becomes active because it takes part in the packet processing instead of limiting itself to simple data routing.

The use of active networks eliminates the need for establishing several multicast trees. Only one tree including all receivers that have subscribed to a video is created (Figure 1). Nevertheless, the subscription list includes information about the required video quality for each subscriber. This information is used by the active nodes to distribute the same video (perhaps a subset of the

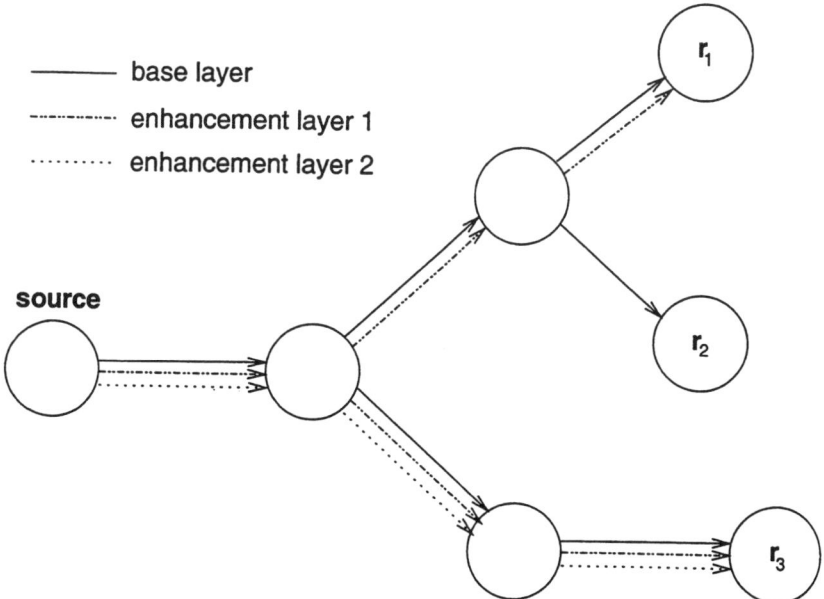

Figure 1. *Multi-layer video transmission in active networks*

layers) through the appropriate outgoing ports. The reader should note that this information is smaller than the one of multiple multicast trees. Therefore, the number of layers of video can be large without overloading the nodes.

3. Multi-source multi-layered video

The advantages of using multicast are challenged by a great number of problems like the routing algorithms in the nodes, the management of the joins/leaves of the various groups, and the computation of the maximum rate of the sources. These problems form a complex system and even more in the case of heterogeneous receivers. In such scenario, either the receivers or the path from the sources to the receivers are limited in resources.[1]

In this work we identify the most important problems related to the multi-source video transmission in heterogeneous multicast networks. First, we are interested in the bandwidth management in the links traversed by more than one video flow. We consider a network in which we have at least one receiver subscribed to different multicast sources, as Figure 2 shows.

If the paths between the sources and the receivers have enough resources to transmit all of the flows, there is no conflict between the flows and they can be normally forwarded. We are interested in the case where at least a link is limited in terms of available bandwidth and the corresponding ingress node must somehow implement a control algorithm. In Figure 2, we consider that source S_1 transmits at a rate d_{s1} and source S_2 at a rate d_{s2}. If the bandwidth bw available in the link is greater than the sum of the rates of the sources, i.e., if $bw > (d_{s1} + d_{s2})$, then we fall into the first case where there is no conflict between the flows. On the other hand, when the sum of the flows exceeds the available bandwidth, then node n_1 must decide how flows will be forwarded to the receivers. We consider a first case where the receivers require 100% of the flows in order to play the video. There are in this case four possibilities of bandwidth allocation:

– $bw < d_{s1}$ and $bw < d_{s2}$: in this case the link does not have enough bandwidth and no flows transported.

– ($bw > d_{s1}$ and $bw < d_{s2}$ or ($bw < d_{s1}$ and $bw > d_{s2}$): only the supported flow is accepted in the link.

– ($bw > d_{s1}$ and $bw > d_{s2}$) but ($bw < d_{s1} + d_{s2}$): only one of the flows can be accepted in the link. The node must implement a priority mechanism.

– $bw > (d_{s1} + d_{s2})$: both flows are accepted in the link.

As multi-layered video is coded in several hierarchical levels, the same source can be viewed as having different rates.[2] We have then more possibilities of resource

---

1. We use here the terminology "network resources" as any resource given to traffic, for example a certain amount of bandwidth, the priority in a queue, etc.
2. We mean a first rate equal to the base layer, the second rate equal to the base layer plus the rate bandwidth of the first enhancement layer and so on.

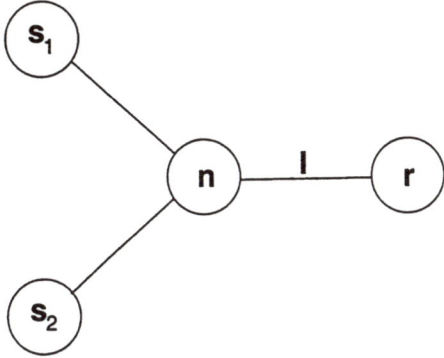

Figure 2. *The multi-source scenario*

allocation since for the same available bandwidth we can admit a more significant number of flows with lower rates, or a reduced number of flows with higher rates.

We suppose in our scheme that each receiver must provide a profile. This profile is a classification by priority of the flows required by a receiver. A change of the profile can occur either in the case of a new subscription to a video source or in the case of a change of priorities. The network of Figure 3 consists of 4 video sources, $S = \{s_1, ..., s_4\}$, and of 3 receivers $R = \{r_1, ..., r_3\}$. Let $F = \{f_1, ..., f_4\}$ be the video flows transmitted respectively by the sources $s_1, ..., s_4$. Each receiver must give its profile based on the hierarchy of the required video flows. Table 1 represents the various profiles of the different receivers in our example.

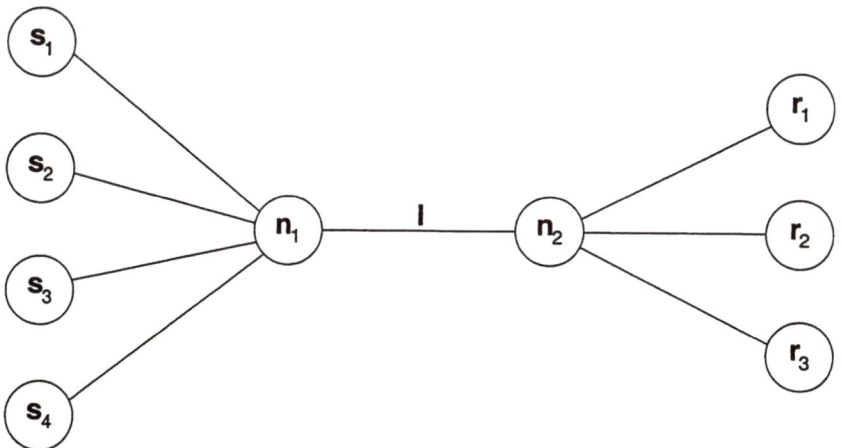

Figure 3. *Multi-source and multi-receiver topology*

Table 1. Flows hierarchy

Receiver	Hierarchy
r_1	$f_1 > f_2 > f_3$
r_2	$f_4 > f_2$
r_3	f_4

We note that receiver r_1 gives the highest priority to the flow f_1, then to f_2, and finally to flow f_3. Receiver r_2 gives the highest priority to flow f_4 and then to flow f_2. In the same way, receiver r_3 requests only the flow f_4 and gives therefore the highest priority to this one.

First, we show that a problem can arise in the links shared by several multicast trees (the link l in Figure 3). To solve this problem, a priority must be established between the different flows traversing this link. Our algorithm consists of giving a weight to each flow at each receiver. This weight, initialized at the number of sources in the network, is a decrement of one every time we go down in the hierarchy of the flows given by the receivers (profile). Therefore, for receiver r_1 the flow f_1 has a weight equal to 4 (since there are 4 sources in the network), a weight of 3 is given to flow f_2, and finally a weight of 2 to flow f_3. Since the receiver r_1 has not subscribed to the multicast tree associated with the source s_4, a weight equal to 0 is allotted to flow f_4. If we apply the same mechanism for all of the other receivers, we have then the different values indicated in Table 2.

Table 2. Weights of the flows in the receivers

Receivers	Weight (P)
r_1	$P(f_1)=4$; $P(f_2)=3$; $P(f_3=2)=2$; $P(f_4)=0$
r_2	$P(f_1)=0$; $P(f_2)=3$; $P(f_3=2)=0$; $P(f_4)=4$
r_3	$P(f_1)=0$; $P(f_2)=0$; $P(f_3=2)=0$; $P(f_4)=4$

The weights of each flow are transmitted downstream towards its source. Each intermediate active node calculates the new weights of the flows by performing a simple sum, for each flow, of the weights received from the different receivers. Therefore, for the nodes n_1 and n_2 we have the weights indicated in Table 3.

Table 3. Weights of the flows in the active nodes

Node	Weight (P)
n_1	$P(f_1)=4$; $P(f_2)=6$; $P(f_3=2)=2$; $P(f_4)=8$
n_2	$P(f_1)=4$; $P(f_2)=6$; $P(f_3=2)=2$; $P(f_4)=8$

In the link l the highest priority is given to the base layer of the flow f_4, then to the base layer of the flow f_2, then the base layer of the flow f_1, and finally to the base layer of the flow f_3. It is the same for the first enhancement layer and so on until the total consumption of the link bandwidth.

4. Analysis

In this paper, we are interested in the performance of a node when this has to manipulate a large number of feedback priority messages with pseudo-random characteristics. We consider the network shown in Figure 4. The topology consists of a set of links L, the set of receivers $R = \{r_k\}_{k \in \{1,M\}}$, and a number of sources $S = \{s_k\}_{k \in \{1,N\}}$, where s_k is the sender of the multicast session m_k.

We suppose one multicast session per video source. On the other side, a receiver r can participate in many multicast sessions. Each receiver r_k must provide a profile classifying the different flows required by this receiver. We define p_{rj}^k, as the weight of flow of the kth multicast session for receiver r_j.

These weights correspond to the priorities of the flows at each one of the receivers and allow the algorithm to classify the different flows in the upstream nodes shared by a number of multicast trees. The computation of the weights depends on the position of the flow in the classification table. To the most important flow, the algorithm gives a weighting p_{rk}^i equal to number of sources in the network. The weighting $p_{rk}^i - 1$ is given to the flow in the second position of the classification table. This is repeated for all flows required by receiver r_k as shows the following equation.

$$p_{r_k}^i = \begin{cases} \# \text{ of sources} & \text{if } i = 1; \\ p_{r_k}^{i-1} - 1 & \text{for the } i\text{th flow required by receiver } r_k; \\ 0 & \text{for the flows not required by receiver } r_k. \end{cases} \qquad [2]$$

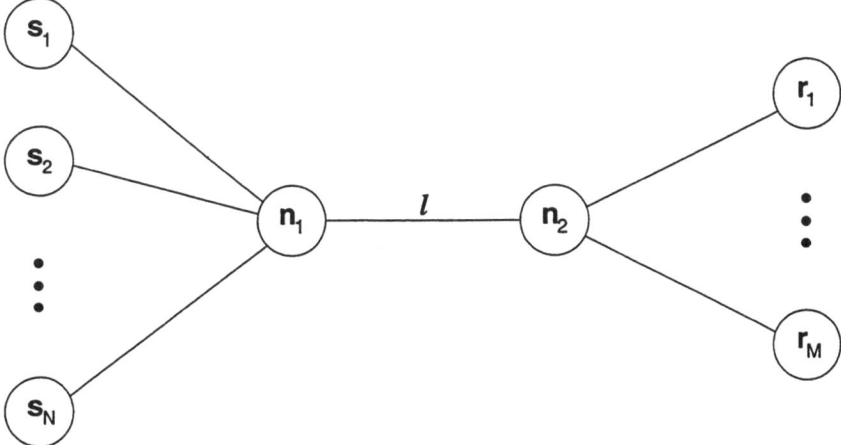

Figure 4. *Analysis topology*

Once the weights have been given to each one of the flows and at each one of the receivers, a vector with all the weights is transmitted to the source. At the reception of the packets sent by downstream nodes, the active intermediate node n merges the correspondent vectors to create a new "combined" classification of the flows. The merging procedure is simple and the resulting vector is obtained through the sum of the weights of each one of the flows, as represented in the equation below.

$$p_n^{f_i} = \sum_{k=1}^{m} p_{r_k}^{f_i},$$ [3]

We have at the intermediate node n a new classification based on the weight obtained from the received vectors. This classification allows the node to fairly allocate the bandwidth of the links shared by different flows. This allocation respects the following rules:

Algorithm 1 Bandwidth Sharing

$i \Leftarrow 1$

$j \Leftarrow 1$

BW_consumed $\Leftarrow 0$

while $(i <= $ Nb_max_sources) **and** $(j <= $ Nb_max_levels) **do**

   if ((BW_consumed + rate(**level** j of **flow** j) $<= $ BW_total) **then**

      Transmission of **level** j of **flow** i

      BW_consumed $\Leftarrow$ BW_consumed+rate(**level** j of **flow** i)

   end if

   $i \Leftarrow i + 1$

   if $i ==$ Nb _max_levels **then**

      $i \Leftarrow 1$

      $j \Leftarrow j + 1$

   end if

end while

We have simulated the topology of Figure 4 with ten three-layer video sources and one hundred receivers. We consider the link l as the bottleneck link, i.e. all of the other links can transmit the required rate without congestion or losses. The capacity of link l is 1 Mbps. For the video sources, each layer has a constant rate of 300 Kbps.

The curve plotted in Figure 5 shows the total amount of bandwidth allocated in the link l. We can observe that almost all of the resources are used, which means an almost optimum bandwidth utilization. Even in the worst case the proposed algorithm results in a bandwidth consumption greater than 85%.

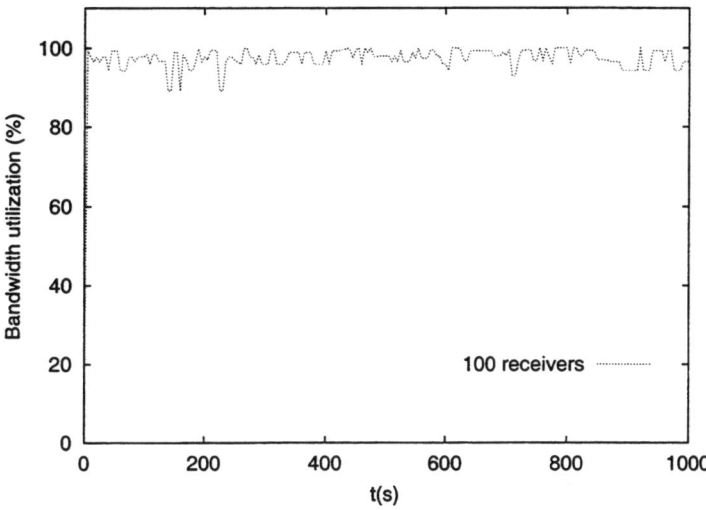

Figure 5. Bandwidth utilization

The second analysis corresponds to the responsiveness of the proposed scheme, and is represented in Figure 6. The corresponding curve shows the number of clients served with at least the base layer of all of the required flows. We note in this graphic the high speed of convergence of the system, with 100% of the clients being quickly served.

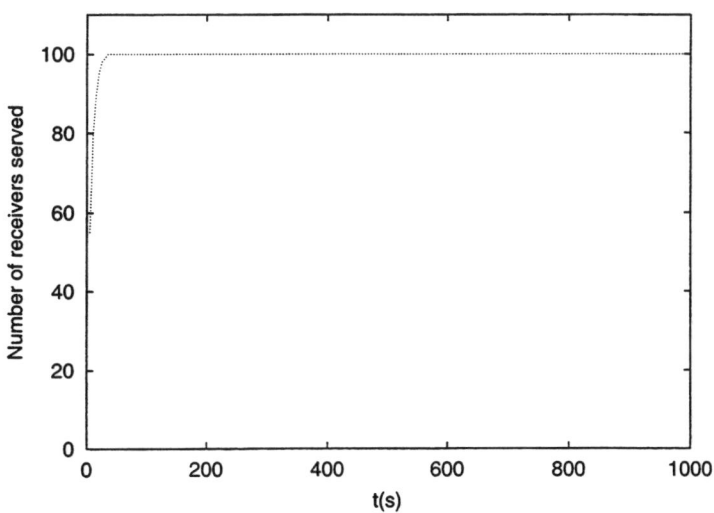

Figure 6. Number of receivers served with at least the base layer

5. Conclusion

We have shown in this paper that an active management of multi-source multicast distribution of multi-layered video offers a better quality of service for the whole set of receivers. Indeed, in this paper we observe that a simple classification at the receivers yields a more efficient distribution of the resources for shared links. The obtained results show that the bandwidth is efficiently allocated and that our proposal leads to fair resource sharing among the multicasts groups. We can note also that this mechanism provides quickly all the clients with at least the base layer, so no receivers are neglected for the benefit of other ones.

Acknowledgement

The authors would like to thank CAPES, COFECUB, UFRJ, and CNRS for their support of this work.

REFERENCES

[ALE 98] ALEXANDER D.S., ARBAUGH W.A., HICKS M.W., KAKKAR P., KEROMYTIS A.D., MOORE J.T., GUNTER C.A., NETTLES S.M., SMITH J.M., "The SwitchWare Active Network Architecture", *IEEE Network Special Issue on Active and Controllable Networks*, vol. 12, 1998, p. 29–36.

[AMO 00] DE AMORIM M.D., DUARTE O.C.M.B., PUJOLLE G., "Multi-Criteria Arguments for Improving the Fairness of Layered Multicast Applications", *Lecture Notes in Computer Science*, vol. 1815, 2000, p. 1–10.

[DEC 98] DECASPER D., PLATTNER B., "DAN: Distributed Code Cashing for Active Networks", *IEEE Infocom'98*, San Francisco, CA, 1998.

[LI 99] LI X., AMMAR M.H., PAUL S., "Video Multicast over the Internet", *IEEE Network Magazine*, 1999.

[NON 99] NONNENMACHER J., BIERSACK E.W., "Scalable Feedback for Large Groups", *IEEE Transactions on Networking*, vol. 7, n° 3, 1999, p. 375–386.

[PSO 99] PSOUNIS K., "Active Networks: Applications, Security, Safety, and Architectures", *IEEE Communications Surveys*, 1999.

[RUB 99] RUBENSTEIN D., KUROSE J., TOWSLEY D., "The Impact of Multicast Layering on Network Fairness", *ACM Sigcomm*, Cambridge, Massachussets, USA, 1999.

[SAP 00] SAPARILLA D., ROSS K.W., "Optimal Streaming of Layered Video", *IEEE Infocom*, Tel-Aviv, Israel, 2000.

[SAR 00] SARKAR S., TASSIULAS L., "Distributed Algorithms for Computation of Fair Rates in Multirate Multicast Trees", *IEEE Infocom*, Tel-Aviv, Israel, 2000.

[TEN 97] TENNENHOUSE D.L., SMITH J.M., SINCOSKIE W.D., WETHERALL J.D., MINDEN G.J., "A Survey of Active Network Research", *IEEE Comunications Magazine*, vol. 35, 1997, p. 80–86.

[WET 98] WETHERALL D., GUTTAG J.V., TENNENHOUSE J.D., "ANTS: A Toolkit for Building and Dynamically Deploying Network Protocols", *IEEE Openarch'98*, San Francisco, CA, 1998.

Index

Innovative Technology Series
Information Systems and Networks

Other titles in this series

Advances in UMTS Technology

Edited by J. C. Bic and E. Bonek
£58.00   1903996147   216 pages   April 2002

The Universal Mobile Telecommunication System (UMTS), the third generation mobile system, is now coming into use in Japan and Europe. The main benefits – spectrum efficient radio interfaces offering high capacity, large bandwidths, ability to interconnect with IP-based networks, and flexibility of mixed services with variable data – offer exciting prospects for the deployment of these networks.

This publication, written by academic researchers, manufacturers and operators, addresses several issues emphasising future evolution to improve the performance of the 3rd generation wireless mobile on to the 4th generation. Outlining as it does key topics in this area of enormous innovation and commercial investment, this material is certain to excite considerable interest in academia and the communications industry.

The content of this book is derived from *Annals of Telecommunications*, published by GET, Direction Scientifique, 46 rue Barrault, F 75634 Paris Cedex 13, France.

Java and Databases

Edited by A. Chaudhri
£35.00   1903996155   136 pages   April 2002

Many modern data applications such as geographical information systems, search engines and computer aided design systems depend on having adequate storage management control. The tools required for this are called persistent storage managers. This book describes the use of the programming language Java in these and other applications.

This publication is based on material presented at a workshop entitled 'Java and Databases: Persistence Options' held in Denver, Colorado in November 1999. The contributions represent the experience acquired by academics, users and practitioners in managing persistent Java objects in their organisations.

For information about other engineering and science titles published by Hermes Penton Science, go to **www.hermespenton.com**

Quantitative Approaches in Object-oriented Software Engineering

Edited by F. Brito e Abreu, G. Poels, H. Sahraoui, H. Zuse
£35.00   1903996279   136 pages   April 2002

Software internal attributes have been extensively used to help software managers, customers and users characterise, assess and improve the quality of software products. Software measures have been adopted to increase understanding of how software internal attributes affect overall software quality, and estimation models based on software measures have been used successfully to perform risk analysis and to assess software maintainability, reusability and reliability. The object-oriented approach presents an advance in technology, providing more powerful design mechanisms and new technologies including OO frameworks, analysis/design patterns, architectures and components. All have been proposed to improve software engineering productivity and software quality.

The key topics in this publication cover metrics collection, quality assessment, metrics validation and process management. The contributors are from leading research establishments in Europe, South America and Canada.

Turbo Codes: Error-correcting Codes of Widening Application

Edited by M. Jézéquel and R. Pyndiah
£50.00   1903996260   206 pages   May 2002

The last ten years have seen the appearance of a new type of correction code – the *turbo code*. This represents a significant development in the field of error-correcting codes.

The decoding principle is to be found in an iterative exchange of information (*extrinsic information*) between elementary decoders. The turbo concept is now applied to block codes as well as other parts of a digital transmission system, such as detection, demodulation and equalisation.

Providing an excellent compromise between complexity and performance, turbo codes have now become a reference in the field, and their range of application is increasing rapidly to mobile communications, interactive television, as well as wireless networks and local radio loops. Future applications could include cable transmission, short distance communication or data storage.

This publication includes contributions from an internationally-based group of authors, from France, Sweden, Australia, USA, Italy, Germany and Norway.

The content of this book is derived from *Annals of Telecommunications*, published by GET, Direction Scientifique, 46 rue Barrault, F 75634 Paris Cedex 13, France.

For information about other engineering and science titles published by Hermes Penton Science, go to **www.hermespenton.com**

Millimeter Waves in Communication Systems

Edited by M. Ney

£50.00   1903996171   180 pages   May 2002

The topics covered in this publication provide a summary of major activities in the development of components, devices and systems in the millimetre-wave range. It shows that solutions have been found for technological processes and design tools needed in the creation of new components. Such developments come in the wake of the demands arising from frequency allocations in this range. The other numerous new applications include satellite communication and local area networks that are able to cope with the ever-increasing demand for faster systems in the telecommunications area.

The content of this book is derived from *Annals of Telecommunications*, published by GET, Direction Scientifique, 46 rue Barrault, F 75634 Paris Cedex 13, France.

Intelligent Agents for Telecommunication Environments

Edited by D. Gaïti and O. Martikainen

£35.00   1903996295   110 pages   June 2002

Telecommunication systems become more dynamic and complex with the introduction of new services, mobility and active networks. The use of artificial intelligence and intelligent agents, integrated reasoning, learning, co-operating and mobility capabilities to provide predictive control are among possible ways forward. There is a need to investigate performance, flow and congestion control, intelligent control environment, security service creation and deployment and mobility of users, terminals and services. New approaches include the introduction of intelligence in nodes and terminal equipment in order to manage and control the protocols, and the introduction of intelligence mobility in the global network. These tools aim to provide the quality of service and adapt the existing infrastructure to be able to handle the new functions and achieve the necessary co-operation between nodes. This book's contributors, who come from research establishments all over the world, address these problems and provide ways forward in this fast-developing area of intelligence in networks.

For information about other engineering and science titles published by Hermes Penton Science, go to **www.hermespenton.com**

Multimedia Management

Edited by J. Neuman de Souza and N. Agoulmine
£40.00   1903996236   140 pages   July 2002

With the arrival of multimedia services via the network, the study of multimedia transmission over various network technologies has been the focus of interest for research teams all over the world.

The previously antagonistic QoS and IP-based network technologies are now part of an integrated approach, which are expected to lead to new intelligent approaches to traffic and congestion control, and to provide the end user with quality service customised multimedia communications. This publication emanates from papers presented at a Multimedia Management conference held in Paris in May 2000.

Applications and Services in Wireless Networks

Edited by H. Afifi and D. Zeghlache
£58.00   1903996309   260 pages   July 2002

Emerging wireless technologies for both public and private use have led to the creation of new applications. These include the adaptation of current network management procedures and protocols and the introduction of unified open service architectures. Aspects such as accounting for multiple media access and QoS (Quality of Service) profiling must also be introduced to enable multimedia service offers, service management and service control over the wireless Internet. Security and content production are needed to foster the development of new services while adaptable applications for variable bandwidth and variable costs will open new possibilities for ubiquitous communications. In this book the contributors, drawn from a broad international field, address these prospects from the most recent perspectives.

For information about other engineering and science titles published by Hermes Penton Science, go to **www.hermespenton.com**

Mobile Agents for Telecommunication Applications

Edited by E. Horlait
£35.00   1903996287   110 pages   July 2002

Mobile agents are concerned with self-contained and identifiable computer programs that can move within a network and can act on behalf of the user and another entity. Most current research work on the mobile agent paradigm has two general goals: the reduction of network traffic and asynchronous interaction, the object being to reduce information overload and to efficiently use network resources. The international contributors to this book provide an overview of how the mobile code can be used in networking with the aim of developing further intelligent information retrieval, network and mobility management, and network services.

Wireless Mobile Phone Access to the Internet

By Thomas Noel
£40.00   1903996325   150 pages   September 2002

Wireless mobile phone access to the Internet will add a new dimension to the way we access information and communicate. This book is devoted to the presentation of recent research on the deployment of the network protocols and services for mobile hosts and wireless communication on the Internet.

A lot of wireless technologies have already appeared: IEEE 802.11b, Bluetooth, HiperLAN/2, GPRS, UTMS. All of them have the same goal: offering wireless connectivity with minimum service disruption between mobile handovers. The mobile world is divided into two parts: firstly, mobile nodes can be attached to several access points when mobiles move around; secondly, ad-hoc networks exist which do not use any infrastructure to communicate. With this model all nodes are mobiles and they cooperate to forward information between each other. This book presents these two methods of Internet access and presents research papers that propose extensions and optimisations to the existing protocols for mobility support.

One can assume that in the near future new mobiles will appear that will support multiple wireless interfaces. Therefore, the new version of the Internet Protocol (IPv6) will be one of the next challenges for the wireless community.

For information about other engineering and science titles published by Hermes Penton Science, go to **www.hermespenton.com**